The Symbolic Order
of the Mother

SUNY series in Contemporary Italian Philosophy

Silvia Benso and Brian Schroeder, editors

The Symbolic Order of the Mother

Luisa Muraro

Translated by
Francesca Novello

Edited and with an Introduction by
Timothy S. Murphy

Foreword by
Alison Stone

Published by State University of New York Press, Albany

© 2018 State University of New York

© 1991, 2006 Editori Riuniti, *L'ordine simbolico della madre*

All rights reserved

No part of this book may be used or reproduced in any manner whatsoever without written permission. No part of this book may be stored in a retrieval system or transmitted in any form or by any means including electronic, electrostatic, magnetic tape, mechanical, photocopying, recording, or otherwise without the prior permission in writing of the publisher.

For information, contact State University of New York Press, Albany, NY
www.sunypress.edu

Production, Ryan Morris
Marketing, Michael Campochiaro

Library of Congress Cataloging-in-Publication Data

Names: Muraro, Luisa, 1940– author. | Murphy, Timothy S., 1964– editor.
Title: The symbolic order of the mother / Luisa Muraro ; translated by Francesca Novello ; edited and with an introduction by Timothy S. Murphy ; foreword by Alison Stone.
Other titles: Ordine simbolico della madre. English
Description: Albany, NY : State University of New York, 2018. | Series: SUNY series in contemporary Italian philosophy | Includes bibliographical references and index.
Identifiers: LCCN 2016059959 (print) | LCCN 2017050116 (ebook) | ISBN 9781438467658 (ebook) | ISBN 9781438467634 (hardcover   ) | ISBN 9781438467641 (pbk.   )
Subjects: LCSH: Mothers. | Identity (Psychology)
Classification: LCC HQ759 (ebook) | LCC HQ759 .M92613 2018 (print) | DDC 306.874/3—dc23
LC record available at https://lccn.loc.gov/2016059959

10 9 8 7 6 5 4 3 2 1

Contents

Foreword *Alison Stone*	vii
Translator's Note *Francesca Novello*	xvii
Introduction: From Separation to Creative Difference *Timothy S. Murphy*	xxiii
Author's Note to the English-Language Edition	xxxi
Preface	xxxiii
Chapter 1 The Difficulty of Beginning	1
Chapter 2 Knowing How to Love the Mother as a Sense of Being	17
Chapter 3 The Word, a Gift from the Mother	35
Chapter 4 Or the One in Her Place	51
Chapter 5 The Circle of Flesh	69
Chapter 6 The Abyssal Distance	85
Notes	99
Index	121

Foreword

Luisa Muraro's book *L'ordine simbolico della madre* was published in 1991 and translated into German in 1993, Spanish in 1994, and French in 2003. The publication of this translation is very welcome; it makes available to English speakers, at last, this important work of Italian feminist philosophy—a singular and affecting book. It has a personal tone, as Muraro leads us through the development of her own thought. She begins by describing her intellectual difficulties and blockages, the problem of how to begin writing, how even to think. She traces the source of these difficulties in the patriarchal culture and philosophy she has inherited, and she gradually elaborates a solution, in the guise of the "symbolic order of the mother."

During this elaboration Muraro draws on a wide range of interlocutors: Irigaray, Kristeva, Hegel, Lacan, and Adrienne Rich among others. As this list indicates, her book speaks to debates about the relations between feminism and psychoanalysis; about the possibilities for a feminism of sexual difference, a project associated particularly but not exclusively with Luce Irigaray; and about motherhood and the maternal. Muraro's book may also be read as a contribution to the development of "continental feminism," the emerging body of work that lies at the intersection of feminist and continental European philosophy.

Above all, Muraro's book is important for its highly original theses regarding the maternal order, theses that have remained little known to Anglophone feminists. So in this foreword I will introduce these theses as I understand them, bearing in mind that there is an open-endedness, and so openness to interpretation, about many of Muraro's key terms. This open-endedness is the inevitable result of Muraro's attempt to articulate matters that patriarchy has left unthought.

Muraro reminds us that our mothers teach us to speak—and often read—in childhood. Our mothers introduce us into language, and thus transmit civilisation: "mothers . . . teach their children to speak and do many other things that are foundations of human civilization" (19). As she insists, Muraro means "mothers" here literally, not metaphorically. But she also says that she speaks of the mother symbolically, which she explains as follows:

> During childhood, we worshipped the mother and all that is related to her, from the husband she had to the shoes she wore, from the sound of her voice to the smell of her skin. We have put her at the center of a magnificent and realistic mythology. I entrust to the little girl I was, to those little girls with whom I grew up, to the little girls and boys who live among us, I entrust to them the task of testifying to the non-metaphorical symbolicity of the mother. (19)

As a "symbolic" figure, then, the mother is invested by us when we are children with an immense wealth of meaning and emotional import. But those who are so invested are our actual, real, literal mothers. This passage, moreover, exemplifies how Muraro draws on personal experience and recollections and imbues them with philosophical significance, moving seamlessly from fragments of life-history to metaphysics—a quality I greatly admire in her book.

Muraro writes of speech as the medium in which we negotiate our early relationships with our mothers: "Language can be given to us only by means of . . . negotiation with the mother because language is nothing other than the fruit of that negotiation" (46). These early relationships are bodily and deeply emotional, so that here the body and the word are completely entwined. In these relationships, too, our mothers have *authority* for us, and to this extent the mother-child relationship is one not of equality but *disparity*, insofar as the mother is our authority, guide, and teacher.

In advancing these claims Muraro is opposing the many psychoanalytic views, including those of Freud and Lacan, according to which the father or father figure, not the mother, embodies law, language, and civilisation, so that we must all break away psychologically and emotionally from our mothers to enter civilisation and become speaking beings. Kristeva, in this vein, claims that "For man and for woman the loss of the mother is a biological and psychic necessity, the first step on the way to autonomy. Matricide is our vital necessity, the *sine qua non* of our individuation" (1989: 38).[1] Muraro agrees with the psychoanalytic tradition, however, on the immense importance of young children's early relationships with their mothers. For Muraro, our early lives are thoroughly relational: at this time, the "subject in relation with the matrix of life . . . is a subject that can be distinguished from the matrix but not from its relation to it. Therefore, it is not exactly a relation between two . . ." (38). Thus, for Muraro, in our childhood relationships with our mothers we are held within this "matrix of life."

Muraro understands the language into which our mothers initiate us in a particular way, as constituting a symbolic order. That is, language is not a neutral tool of communication; rather, each language embodies a determinate horizon of meanings, which we take on in learning to speak. Indeed, more strongly still, Muraro regards language as the medium through which the world reveals itself to us, becoming manifest in a determinate shape. It is not, then, that language cuts us off from the world as it might really be; instead, language is the condition of the world's appearing to us and becoming known by us at all. To enter language, and so for the world to present itself to us in a specific way, is to enter the realm of *truth*, for Muraro: truth as the self-revelation or self-manifestation of the world, which precedes and makes possible truth as correspondence.[2]

Thus, by connecting her claims about the mother's early importance, and her importance with respect to speech and language in particular, with her theses about the world-manifesting character of language, Muraro comes to attribute a very far-reaching role to the mother. In inducting each of us into speech, the mother equally enfolds us into a culture, a world, and the interwoven domains of meaning and truth. The mother makes the world, as a meaningful world, available to us, and we participate in it under her aegis, with the stamp of her authority and person pervading our basic way of experiencing life.

Inescapably, though, our mothers enlist us into *particular* languages and their corresponding horizons of meaning, which each divide up and categorize the world's furniture differently. As a result, there is necessarily an "abyssal" distance, as Muraro puts it (ch. 6), between words and experience—where "experience" means not a private inner set of representations but our direct, lived, bodily relationship with the world as it manifests itself to us. To paraphrase Muraro's thinking here:

languages come to us already embodying specific ways of seeing things that never perfectly fit with, and may diverge more or less markedly from, the particular experiences we have. But that gap or divergence is the key to languages being alive, as we speak in ways with which we attempt to articulate and verbalize our experiences—to close the "abyssal" gap, *per impossibile*. Through our attempts, the languages we inhabit continually evolve.

Overall, Muraro conceives of language as a "mediation"—it mediates our experience and our relationships with the mother, and with others. But the function of a mediation is to mediate what is immediate (experience)—to *restore* what is immediate to us, not to constitute a self-contained sphere cut off from experiential presence (76–77). Likewise, language as the medium in which *any* speaker can speak to any other speaker—a universal medium of social exchange—substitutes for the early exchanges in which we spoke only with our mothers. But, for Muraro, the role of a substitute is to restore to us, and prolong our contact with, that which undergoes substitution, namely the mother. The function of language, then, is not to displace but to extend the mother-child bond.

Nonetheless, the inescapable gap between words and experience is the basis on which it becomes possible for a language to come to form an order set against, and separated from, experience. This has happened, for Muraro, with the patriarchal symbolic order that has long obtained in the West. Muraro diagnoses the problems of this order by recounting her difficult relations with philosophy over the years. She was drawn to the philosophical tradition, she suggests, because it resonated with the aversion she had formed to her mother. Philosophy had this resonance due to its maleness (or, at least, that of the canon of male philosophers) and, above all, due to philosophy's refusal to accept anything as given without question, a refusal enshrined in philosophers' moves to doubt, bracket, or relegate to mere appearance the sensory world (in Descartes, Husserl, and Plato, respectively). This distancing from given reality tied in with Muraro's turn against her mother, she suggests, because in making that turn she at once cut herself off from that intimate, living entwinement of given, bodily experience with language, meaning, and truth which was structured and suffused by her early relationship with her mother (this complex constituting the "matrix of life" in the fuller meaning of that phrase).

Philosophy, then, has according to Muraro been complicit with a symbolic order that has demanded that we turn against our mothers, and has separated word from body and aligned the word, civilization, authority, and power with the father—as in much of psychoanalysis. To be sure, this demand for separation from the mother has not always been explicitly stated (Kristeva notwithstanding), but rather has existed as "a schema underlying a whole way of feeling and acting" (8), in which we turn against our mothers in hostility or silent distance. Nonetheless, it remains our mothers who transmit language to us, but the language they transmit embodies patriarchal demands and denies mothers the very authority and power that they exercise in transmitting it.

However, it is not *necessary* that the symbolic order should be patriarchal and antimaternal, Muraro insists. Contingently, our civilization in the West has been that way, but this can be changed: the symbolic order can be the object of political interventions and practices, ones that we can make intentionally with a view to bringing about change; we need not remain hapless subjects of the symbolic but can exercise agency with respect to it. But what specific changes are we to make?

First and foremost, Muraro maintains, we need to recover our early love for our mothers, and, more broadly, regain something of our way of existing in the world when we were little children. Poignantly, she writes, we need to "freely give meaning to female grandeur, like that of my mother which I experienced and fully recognized in the first months and years of my life, and later on sadly lost and almost repudiated" (20). But it is not a matter only of changing our individual relationships with or attitudes toward our mothers. More broadly, we need to "translate into our adult lives the early relationship with the mother in order to experience it again as the principle of symbolic authority" (32). That is, we are to change the whole structure of our social relationships; perhaps, in part, this entails women placing themselves under the authority, guidance, and tutelage of senior women who are to serve for them as mother figures, substitute mothers. That, at least, was the strategy of *affidamento*—entrustment of one woman to another as her mentor and guide—which was promulgated in the 1983 pamphlet "More Women than Men" by the Milan Women's Bookstore Collective, of which Muraro was a leading member. But to remain with *The Symbolic Order of the Mother*, Muraro also urges that we try to put our experiences into speech, and to reconnect word and body—as in the practice of *autocoscienza* (consciousness-raising), which takes on an expanded significance here. It becomes a means not only of women discovering shared injustices but also of fostering and recapturing the childhood unity of language and experience, the "sense of being" or "matrix of life." At the center of all these strategies, though, Muraro places the need for an emotional reorientation toward love for and not hostility to our mothers as real-life persons, and she advocates recapturing that love in its early, reverential, all-encompassing sense.

There is a great deal in Muraro's rich book that I have omitted from this summary. Muraro has highly suggestive things to say about Marx, Kant, Plato, presence, critique, Jane Austen, mother-daughter relationships, nihilism, hysteria, and much more. And I have not done justice to the character of her writing. As I mentioned before, she weaves deftly between the personal and the metaphysical, and she boldly elevates her own feelings and experiences to philosophical significance, and takes them as a basis from which to revisit a wealth of theoretical work.

Critical discussion of Muraro's ideas, and those of the Milan Women's Bookstore Collective, has focused hitherto on the anti-egalitarianism of Muraro's positive view of authority.[3] While it would be out of place to pursue here in any depth the questions raised by Muraro's claims, I do want to note two questions (and to move beyond the critical preoccupation with equality). First, is it *necessary* that we must learn language from our mothers? Muraro suggests that this is necessary; to recall, she states that "language can be given to us *only* by means of . . . negotiation with the mother because language is *nothing other* than the fruit of that negotiation" (46; my emphases). But, one might reply, surely in fact we learn to speak from our mothers only because, in contingent fact, we have historically had a social division of labor that allocates the care of young children primarily or exclusively to women, while reserving the higher-ranked spheres of public work and politics for men. This gender division of labor has been bound up with the hierarchical division between public and private spheres and, in turn, with the symbolic divisions between civilization and nature, word and body—divisions that Muraro contests. Yet this suggests that the mother has her symbolic authority in teaching us language *only under* a symbolic order that denies her that same authority by dividing maternal body from paternal word, maternal home from patriarchal polity, and so on. In that case, the mother's symbolic authority would be bound up with the patriarchal order that Muraro opposes; to oppose that order consistently, we would have to oppose the (unrecognized but real) symbolic order of the mother too. For if we wish women to participate in public life on an equal footing with men, and for men to participate in childcare no less fully than women, then the mother would have to lose her special authority and presence for young children—to share it with the father, just as men also would have to relinquish their traditional privileges and prerogatives.[4]

Second, Muraro's symbolic order of the mother may be an order of the mother *as seen by the daughter*. To explain: Muraro says that we learn to speak from the mother or "the one in her place" (40). This phrase is at the crux of several issues.[5] Muraro expands on it by speaking of the "symbolic predisposition of the mother [that] also allows others to substitute for her without . . . damaging the work of creation of the world that she accomplishes with her child" (52). Every mother, Muraro then says, is *already* a substitute—for her own mother. "[A] woman . . . always remains the daughter of her mother, so that every natural mother is already a substitute" (52). To teach one's child to speak is to teach them the language one learned in one's childhood from one's own mother. Thus, to perform this role, a mother must carry forward her own mother's lessons, and her acceptance of her own mother's authority is presupposed as she does this. To accept that authority is for a mother to place herself under her own mother's aegis, as her daughter, who is speaking with the child—on Muraro's account of substitution and mediation—as a prolongation of her original speech with her own mother. To act in the capacity of a mother, then, one must occupy the psychical, linguistic, and symbolic position of the *daughter* of one's own mother.

My concern, then, is that Muraro's symbolic order of the mother may, ironically, be an order in which mothers can speak only from the position of daughters, but which allows women no possibility of speaking *as* mothers, from any specifically maternal vantage point. But the mother, for Muraro, teaches us to speak and does so by speaking with us. If the mother is really to exercise power and authority in doing so, and to embody a continuity of body and word, she must ultimately be able to speak in a maternal voice, as a maternal subject. Yet I am not sure whether this is possible within Muraro's framework.

Still, this question of maternal subjectivity is opened up by Muraro's own theses regarding the symbolic order of the mother, which are important not least because there is much truth in them, or so I believe. Specifically, I submit, Muraro is right that—at least given the long-running gender division of labor—the mother brings the child into speech and animates a vital matrix of life in which the young child lives. Muraro is right, therefore, to see the mother as the principal civilizing agent and to find it rather ironic that psychoanalytic tradition has insistently denied her this role and arrogated it to the father. And Muraro is also right (in my view) that that denial forms part of the patriarchal symbolic order which has rested on a rejection of this original maternal authority, but this order can be changed, where this change should begin with and issue from our emotional reorientation to love our mothers. I am less sure that we can reject patriarchy and retain maternal authority, or that this kind of maternal authority is compatible with mothers speaking in a maternal voice. But these are questions that Muraro's invaluable work can help us to think through. With the publication of this translation, English-speaking readers will at last be able to engage with Muraro's ideas and think through their possibilities and implications.

Alison Stone
Lancaster University

Notes

1. However, Muraro also makes central use of Kristeva's conception of the semiotic, the realm of intimate and already significant body-to-body relationships between mother and infant. Whereas for Kristeva the symbolic involves a break from the semiotic (an always incomplete break, though), for Muraro the semiotic in principle extends continuously into the symbolic, albeit that our patriarchal symbolic order—in contingent fact—attempts that kind of break.

2. Muraro is informed by Heidegger, for whom truth as disclosure or unconcealment precedes truth as correspondence of judgments to states of affairs: there must first be a world of meaning to make any individual instances of such correspondence possible. It is arguable, though, that truth just *means* correspondence, so that what Heidegger and Muraro are talking about is something else.

3. See, for example, Re (2002).

4. Significantly, Muraro discusses Evelyn Fox Keller's account of how children come to turn against their mothers and idealize their fathers given conditions of female-exclusive mothering that motivate a reaction against maternal power (Keller in turn is informed by Nancy Chodorow [1978], among others). But, Muraro says, the problem is not social or psychological but symbolic: children only effect this hostile turn because the symbolic order does not confirm or validate their experience of maternal power, but locates authority instead in the father (88). Thus, Muraro does not see the need for shared parenting, which is Keller's (and Chodorow's) proposed solution.

5. Presumably these substitutes can include fathers, grandmothers, neighbors, nannies, day-care workers, and any others to whom the mother delegates care of her child. But the more such delegation goes on, the more the mother resembles after all a metaphor or function—that of inducting the child into speech—which manifold people and agencies may perform. New modes of reproduction in which genetic, gestational, and postnatal motherhood can come apart—not to mention adoption—also present potential complications for Muraro's notion of the "natural mother."

Works Cited

Chodorow, Nancy. 1978. *The Reproduction of Mothering*. Berkeley, CA: University of California Press.

Fox Keller, Evelyn. 1985. *Reflections on Gender and Science*. New Haven, CT: Yale University Press.

Kristeva, Julia. 1989. *Black Sun: Depression and Melancholia*. Trans. Léon S. Roudiez. New York: Columbia University Press.

Re, Lucia. 2002. Diotima's Dilemmas: Authorship, Authority, Authoritarianism. In *Italian Feminist Theory and Practice: Equality and Sexual Difference*, ed. Graziella Parati and Rebecca West, 50–74. London: Associated University Presses.

Translator's Note

FRANCESCA NOVELLO

These pages are not notes on the linguistic challenge of translating or on the difficulty of rendering specific words from Italian into English. I chose not to write about the process of translating, because from the first draft of my translation to its final version there has been a lapse of twenty-three years. I would like to specify, though, that the actual translation of the book has not taken twenty-three years. To be precise, there have been two phases of this translation. The first phase was when I actually translated the book for the first time twenty-three years ago as my master's thesis. Regarding this phase, I don't remember much of the specific difficulties I faced while translating, except for the general challenge of translating from my first language into my second language while being pregnant in the hot months of the Oklahoma summer, under the pressure of finishing and defending my thesis before giving birth to my son. The second phase started last March, when I returned to my thesis project thanks to a number of fortuitous, and lucky, circumstances. Regarding this phase, I don't feel there are many linguistic challenges to point out except for the difficulty of restarting the engine, that is to say my work as a translator, and getting reacquainted with the project after twenty-three dormant years.

It has definitely been a long journey for *The Symbolic Order of the Mother* to reach an English-speaking audience after almost a quarter of a century. And it is for this exact reason that I feel I owe an explanation of why the translation underwent such a circuitous course and delayed publication. Therefore, my translator's notes are, instead, the story of the vicissitudes of this translation in its journey toward its publication and of my gratitude to all the friends and family who helped me keep the project alive by reminding me of the importance of the book and of its publication.

I will start by saying, as I already mentioned, that the translation with my introduction to Muraro's book was my master's thesis for the English Department at the University of Oklahoma. I came across *The Symbolic Order of the Mother* by pure chance. Once I completed my required course work, I felt that I had less clarity about my academic interests and less desire to go on with my studies, and possibly with an academic career later on. I can explicitly say that the lack of a harmonious academic environment in the department eventually led me to lose interest in, not to mention passion for, what I had been studying up to that point. My lack of motivation pushed me to take two semesters off in order to find the drive that could help me rekindle my interest and make me finish the studies I had started with such enthusiasm.

Somehow I still wanted to finish my MA, so I consulted the fall 1993 student's catalog for a new direction of studies, maybe for a different outlook. So it was by chance that I decided to enroll in something quite different from the classes on Medieval studies I had been taking, which I still loved but with much less energy. Susan Green offered a class on feminism. I don't remember the exact title of the course, but that does not matter. What matters instead is what the class made me aware of and ultimately made me want to know more about. We read books by various feminists, and it was during this time that I came across the Milan Women's Bookstore Collective. I wanted to know more about it—its work and its politics of women back home in my country from which I was geographically and culturally very distant and very disconnected as a consequence of living in an area as insular and remote as Oklahoma.

At that time my friend Angelo Cozzo lived in Milan, working as a fashion photographer. I asked him if he could go to the Milan Women's Bookstore to buy and ship to me *Mettere al Mondo il Mondo*. He told me that the bookstore saleswoman recommended that he add *L'Ordine Simbolico della Madre* to his shopping cart, so he did and sent both books to me. I thank him very dearly for having listened to her recommendation and for having given me such a gift.

Reading *L'ordine simbolico della madre* was like a rebirth. The book had brought me into a new world—not just a new academic world but a new world in a holistic sense, a new reality altogether. I deeply thank Luisa Muraro for having opened to me a door into the academic world at a time when my desire to go on was at a standstill. I thank her for having helped me believe in graduate school again at a time when my interest had lost its sense of direction. I thank both her and Susan Green for having rekindled my academic enthusiasm, which allowed me to finish—an opportunity that, at the time, some other dear friends of mine who, like me, had lost their sense of direction did not have and so preferred to move on to other careers and never finished. I am grateful to Luisa Muraro and Susan Green for showing me a different lens through which I could look at the world, at women, at their *reality*; that is, for bringing me to a new awareness. And I also thank Luisa Muraro for randomly mentioning on the first page of her book, of all places in the world, Palermo, the city where I was born, where I grew up, and also New York, the city I love, the city where my son lives, the final destination of her book.

I also thank my MA committee, composed of Susan Green, Ronald Schleifer, and Catherine Hobbs, for having supported me throughout the completion of the initial translation and for their valuable suggestions and editing work. I particularly want to thank Ronald Schleifer, who patiently pursued the publication of my thesis as a valuable book twenty-three years ago. Even though the publication fell through because of internal conflicts at the publishing house, I remain grateful to Ron Schleifer for his support and his endless efforts to make the publication of Muraro's book happen.

The end of my thesis coincided with the end of my pregnancy. This marked the beginning of years of health issues. The childbirth was difficult and life threatening. My son was in intensive care and I remained debilitated for quite some time. A few years later I was diagnosed with breast cancer, and then after treatment I was diagnosed with it yet again. All of this went on for ten years. Surgeries and treatment ultimately, and rightly so, distanced me more and more from my translation. But it was during those years that, on and off, dear friends from the academic world reminded me of my translation of Muraro's book and that it must be published. On many occasions I was contacted by students from various parts of the world who were interested in working with my translation and who encouraged me to have it published. It was during those difficult times that my friend Susan Laird never stopped reminding me of my project and of the importance of revising the translation in order to pursue its publication. I thank her for her support, and for always reminding me that I needed to go back to work on my translation and that my project was valuable. I thank Susan Laird for keeping the desire to return to the project present in my mind even when times were difficult. But at that time my health was my only immediate concern and my true priority.

When my health was good again and hard times had passed, I knew I had to go back to my project, but how to start the engine again? So much time had passed. There was so much temporal distance between me and the translation. Then one day I got in touch with Tim Murphy, with whom I had done a translation of a couple of essays by Toni Negri before my first diagnosis. I needed a letter of reference for a new job position in our department, so I asked him if he would write it for me. On that occasion he asked me if I was still thinking of going back to my translation in order to have it published. Thanks to his support, my translation was accepted for publication by SUNY Press, to whom I am also grateful. Since then, Tim Murphy's help and guidance throughout the revision of the initial translation has been a valuable, supportive, and encouraging learning process. His patience, enthusiasm, support, and hard work will never be forgotten. I am very grateful and thankful to Tim Murphy for having made a dream come true. Without him, *The Symbolic Order of the Mother* would have probably never been published in English.

From the moment the revision of the initial translation started, several people have contributed to the completion of the final version. First of all, I want to thank my friend Andrea L'Afflitto, who scanned the original document of my translation from disks into Microsoft Word and made the document readable in an electronic format. I thank Andrea for his valuable help.

Going back to the translation required many weeks of revisions that Tim Murphy and I did together. It was during those weeks of revisions that my friends Lori Bacigalupi and Mary Doezema gave me their friendship and their support during our tea and coffee breaks, which I always looked forward to. I thank them for their love and for their supportive words in the course of the revision of my translation. Their friendship added further vigor to my involvement with the project. I also want to thank my friends Patrizia La Vecchia and Giovanni Massa, in Palermo, who helped me locate a few quotations from Italian books that either did not have an English edition or were hard to find in their corresponding English versions. I know that this meant for them facing the anarchic traffic in the chaotic city of Palermo, in order to reach the university libraries that owned those books. I thank them dearly. My friend Maurizio Vito gave me good advice at the very beginning of the revision and, while on vacation in Corfu, helped me (thanks to WhatsApp) with a couple of Italian sentences that seemed ambiguous to me. Thank you, Maurizio.

Last, I want to thank my husband Nasir and my son Mir always for having been supportive of me, of my work, and of my possibilities. Their love and warm words of encouragement have helped me endure hard times and fueled my desire and determination to finally finish a project that started twenty-three years ago. I also thank my mother, Anna, for supporting me in bringing this project to completion by accepting that I had to renounce my annual visit to her this past summer. I thank my mother for being my mother, for always being there for me.

Introduction

From Separation to Creative Difference

TIMOTHY S. MURPHY

I would like to thank Francesca Novello for allowing me to contribute to this translation, Martin Wallen for helping track down quotations, and my wife Juliana for keeping me focused. As always, Silvia Benso, Brian Schroeder, and Andrew Kenyon of SUNY Press did everything possible to speed this project to its conclusion. Any errors or oversights that remain are Francesca's and my responsibility.

Luisa Muraro is one of the most inventive, influential, and intransigent thinkers to emerge from the vast panorama of Italian feminism since 1968, yet this is the first of her books to be translated into English.[1] The tremendous proliferation of translations from contemporary Italian philosophy since 2000, which has broadened the range of Italian thought available to English-speaking readers to a degree almost unimaginable only a few years earlier, nevertheless has not kept pace with such unique developments within Italian feminism. Thus some background is in order.

The sixth of eleven children, Muraro was born in 1940 in Montecchio Maggiore, in the province of Vicenza, part of the Veneto region. Her father was a decorated anti-Fascist partisan during the Second World War. She attended the Catholic University of Louvain in Belgium and the Università Cattolica del Sacro Cuore di Gesù [Catholic University of the Sacred Heart of Jesus] in Milan, where she originally studied modern languages and linguistics before switching to philosophy under the mentorship of the neo-Aristotelian philosopher Gustavo Bontadini, as she notes in chapters 1 and 2 below. Some of her earliest publications focused on Saussurean linguistics, and the Swiss thinker's work continues to be an important point of reference for her. During the tumultuous early 1970s, Muraro collaborated with Elvio Fachinelli and Lea Melandri on the counterculture journal *L'erba voglio* [*The "I Want" Plant*], but the turning point in her career as an intellectual and activist came in 1975, when she cofounded the Libreria delle Donne di Milano [the Milan Women's Bookstore] along with Lia Cigarini and others. Although Muraro taught in the philosophy department of the University of Verona from 1976 to 2006, the rigid structure of Italian universities effectively precluded the institutionalization of women's studies programs during much of that period, and indeed some Italian feminists were openly wary of such institutionalization, suspecting that it would result in ghettoization. Consequently, independent organizations like the Milan Women's Bookstore played a crucial role in providing space—physical, social, and intellectual—for the development of the burgeoning women's movement in Italy. Although the Milan Women's Bookstore still operates, and one volume of writings by women involved in its operation has been translated into English (titled *Sexual Difference*),[2] Muraro has focused her attention since 1984 on the work of the female philosophical community Diotima, which she cofounded that year with the philosopher Adriana Cavarero, among others, and which is currently affiliated with the University of Verona. The community is named for Diotima of Mantinea, the Greek priestess to whom Socrates attributes the articulation of the doctrine of love that leads from admiration for individual beauty to the contemplation of beauty in itself, and ultimately to the reverence for the intelligible world of Forms in Plato's *Symposium*.

Muraro has been the most productive and outspoken member of both the Milan Women's Bookstore collective and the Diotima community since their respective inceptions. Her influence as a thinker and writer is at least threefold. First, she is the primary Italian translator of the well-known Belgian-French feminist philosopher Luce Irigaray, whose work partially inspired Muraro's own and who engaged in a fertile exchange of ideas with the women of the Diotima community for many years. Second, Muraro has been a key figure in the recovery of what she calls "female genealogies," the often fragmentary and overwritten signs of women's theological, philosophical, and psychological invention that Western patriarchal culture has suppressed over the past two millennia or more.[3] For example, she has done extensive research into the persecution of witches in medieval and early modern Europe[4] and into the phenomena of female religious mysticism and female heresy.[5] Third, she is a highly original philosopher, indeed a self-professed metaphysician, in her own right, and this is the aspect of her work that justifies this translation.

The rationale and practices of the Diotima community reveal the unique characteristics of Muraro's (and her colleagues') feminism. It draws from the broader currents of Italian feminism an emphasis on consciousness-raising, which was originally borrowed from American second-wave practice, translated by the great polemicist Carla Lonzi as *autocoscienza* (literally "self-consciousness"), and transformed from a collective analysis of patriarchal oppression into "a process of the discovery and (re-)construction of the self, both the self of the individual woman and a collective sense of self."[6] This reconstruction demanded a systematic, though not absolute or permanent, separation from patriarchal relationships and institutions, hence the importance of creating women's spaces like bookstores and co-ops as well as means of communication like independent journals and presses. More importantly, it also demanded the establishment of new relationships among women themselves, relationships of *affidamento* or "entrustment" to replace the relations of rivalry, resentment, or commiseration encouraged by patriarchy. These three elements of *autocoscienza*, separatism, and *affidamento* are shared by many of the groups that make up the constellation of Italian feminism.

More specific to the Diotima community (and Muraro) are dissatisfaction with and resistance to the politics of equality that dominate Anglo-American feminist practice. Again following Lonzi,[7] the members of the Diotima community understand political equality to mean the abstract universality of subjects who appear as neuter and indifferent before the law, which nevertheless defines that universality as essentially male. Thus a politics of women must be a politics of sexual difference, that is, a politics that starts from an acknowledgment of the originary nonuniversality of sexuated subjectivity and experience. That politics in turn can only be based on a thought of sexual difference, the articulation of which is the task that the members of the Diotima community (including Muraro) have set themselves over the past thirty years. Like the Milan Women's Bookstore volume *Sexual Difference*, *The Symbolic Order of the Mother* (originally published in Italian in 1991, and already translated into French, German, and Spanish) is one of the most important and influential contributions to that articulation.

We could enter Muraro's metaphysics by any number of routes. Perhaps the most instructive would be through the figure of Diotima of Mantinea herself. She constitutes a female progenitor formally acknowledged by patriarchal philosophy, but her contributions to thought are expropriated and suppressed by that very acknowledgment. Specifically, the Socratic method of maieutic, whereby the philosopher acts as a "midwife" to his interlocutors by asking questions that do not impart wisdom but instead reveal the truths already contained within the soul, constitutes the originary expropriation of the mother's power to give both life and language (the medium of thought) to the child. Muraro's project in *The Symbolic Order of the Mother* is to restore that power by analyzing and dismantling the terms of the expropriation. Unlike Cavarero, however, who pursues a parallel project in much of her work,[8] Muraro does not adopt a version of the deconstructive method whereby the canonical texts of the patriarchal tradition are submitted to meticulous close reading in order to reveal the insidious pattern of elision, erasure, and paradox that has excluded women from philosophy and the social. Indeed, Muraro explicitly rejects the practice of interminable critique characteristic of deconstruction in favor of a metaphysics of affirmation. She engages the patriarchal tradition obliquely by narrating the blockage that resulted when, as a student, she tried to use traditional philosophy as a means to "invalidate the authority and work of the mother" (6). The canonical figures of Plato, Aristotle, Descartes, Kant, Hegel, Husserl, and Heidegger frame this failed effort, constituting a negative foundation for her own original thinking, which she constructs instead out of elements drawn from a huge range of disciplines and discourses: female mysticism and theology (Marguerite Porete, Simone Weil, Edith Stein), semiotics (Saussure, Roman Jakobson, Charles Sanders Peirce), psychoanalysis (Freud, Lacan, D. W. Winnicott, Melanie Klein), political economy (Marx, Fernand Braudel), world literature (Jane Austen, Clarice Lispector), Anglo-American feminism (Adrienne Rich, Carolyn Heilbrun, Evelyn Fox Keller), and French feminism (Irigaray, Julia Kristeva).

The originary insight that allows Muraro to begin both her affirmative project of metaphysical reconstruction and her book is her recognition of the need to reconnect thinking itself to the love for the mother that everyone experiences during early childhood, when the mother and child together create the world anew through corporeal development and language acquisition. She calls this "knowing how to love the mother" ["*sapere amare la madre*"]. This is not a metaphor, as both the philosophical tradition and some quarters of the feminist movement have it, but in fact an unabashedly ontological claim. The advent of patriarchal law, reexperienced by every child as he or she grows up, shatters, devalues, and ultimately replaces the love for the mother, thereby instituting a symbolic disorder that generates both individual and collective psychopathologies, particularly among women. Such disorder can be seen in the nihilist devaluation of the material world—often gendered female within patriarchy—that underpins idealist philosophy from Plato to Kant and Hegel, for example. This disorder afflicts women especially by blocking access to language and the sayable, but language can be restored by reentering the symbolic order of the mother that patriarchy seeks to suppress. This does not mean regressing to childhood, but rather negotiating a revived relationship with the maternal continuum with which daughters have a privileged connection. Indeed, the symbolic order of the mother is not a biological or biographical relationship between autonomous individuals but instead a structural relation among interdependent beings, which is why the role of the mother can be played effectively by substitutes: whoever works together with the child to construct the body and the faculty of language can legitimately occupy the place of the mother.

Muraro's demonstration of this restorative process passes by way of a rethinking of fixation and hysteria, female neuroses par excellence, a redefinition of the link between logical and factual necessity and between mediation and immediacy, and an extended meditation on the similarities between language and money. The process culminates in a call for a shift in power away from the symbolic disorder of patriarchy, a separation that will make possible a restoration of the symbolic order of the mother, hence a shift that will necessarily be revolutionary in its consequences. That revolution must begin in a reimagining of and struggle over what is sayable, and it can be accomplished only by rigorously following out the implications of restoring sayability to the maternal order, and consequently to women's subjectivity and experience. This, for Muraro, is the only way to achieve women's freedom on their own terms, and not simply as an expansion of the patriarchal logic of abstract political equality.

Muraro's work has been controversial, both within Italy and abroad. Like Irigaray, she has been accused of essentialism in her conceptualization of sexual difference and the mother-child relation, and her theorization and practice of what she calls the "authority of vertical disparity" among women,[9] which promotes the mentorship of young and/or inexperienced women by older, more accomplished women, has sometimes been labeled crypto-authoritarian.[10] No doubt such controversies have contributed to the reluctance on the part of English-language editors and publishers to translate her books. On the other hand, she has also been celebrated as one of the most original and important Italian thinkers of the past century, for example by the equally controversial materialist philosopher Antonio Negri. In his polemical pamphlet "The Italian Difference," Negri insists that Italy has only produced three genuine philosophical innovations during the twentieth century: first of all Antonio Gramsci's philosophy of praxis, subsequently canonized as the ideology of the Italian Communist Party and consequently tarnished by that party's corruption and collapse, and more recently Mario Tronti's workerism [*operaismo*] and Muraro's thought of sexual difference. Negri specifically celebrates those elements of Muraro's thinking that other critics have attacked: her continuing emphasis on women's separatism as the precondition for a politics of difference; her strict differentiation of disparate female "authority" from hierarchical male "power"; and her strong metaphysical affirmation of the mother-child couple's creativity expressed through the body and language (an affirmation which, in Negri's view, far surpasses the "weak thought" of Gianni Vattimo and Pier Aldo Rovatti, and perhaps also the "bare life" of Giorgio Agamben).[11] Regarding the impact of Muraro's metaphysics on political struggles in Italy and around the world, he concludes:

> Over an exceedingly short period of time, Italy experienced the passage from the *separatist* affirmation of difference to its *constituent* affirmation. In fact, these diverse theories of difference did not simply represent a resistance to oppression and the oppressor: they were not entrenched in defensive positions, but became resistance that is productive; they showed that they were a manifold guerrilla movement. Here,

there was no longer simply a theory, but a transformative practice. The practices embedded themselves in the junctures of social communication, threatened in micropolitical forms the major directives of capitalist and patriarchal command, carried out raids into knowledge and the universities, factories and workplaces, families and general social relations. Separation . . . turns into a *creative difference*.[12]

The creative sexual difference exemplified as well as theorized by Muraro's thought gives both women and men something more to say, to do, and to be than they had available to them under the symbolic disorder of patriarchy. If this translation can help to further expand the range of being, doing, and saying, then it will have succeeded in its aim.

Notes

1. A number of her essays have appeared in English-language journals and collections, however, including "Toward a Symbolic of Sexual Difference," trans. Silvia Benso, in the inaugural volume of SUNY Press's Contemporary Italian Philosophy series, *Contemporary Italian Philosophy: Crossing the Borders of Ethics, Politics and Religion*, ed. Silvia Benso and Brian Schroeder (Albany: SUNY Press, 2007), pp. 211–26.

2. Milan Women's Bookstore Collective, *Sexual Difference: A Theory of Social-Symbolic Practice*, trans. Patricia Cicogna and Teresa de Lauretis (Bloomington: Indiana University Press, 1990). Short texts by members of the collective can be found in Paola Bono and Sandra Kemp, eds., *Italian Feminist Thought: A Reader* (Oxford: Blackwell, 1991), pp. 109–38, 329–34.

3. See Muraro's essay "Female Genealogies," trans. Patricia Cicogna and Margaret Whitford, in *Engaging with Irigaray: Feminist Philosophy and Modern European Thought* (New York: Columbia University Press, 1994), pp. 317–33, which also registers the limits of her agreement with Irigaray regarding the struggle with patriarchy.

4. See *La Signora del gioco: Episodi della caccia alle streghe* [*The Lady of the Game: Episodes from the Witch Hunt*] (Milan: Feltrinelli, 1976), reissued by La Tartaruga in 2006.

5. See *Guglielma e Maifreda: Storia di un'eresia femminista* [*Guglielma and Maifreda: Story of a Feminist Heresy*] (Milan: La Tartaruga, 1985); *Lingua materna scienza divina: Scritti sulla filosofia mistica di Margherita Porete* [*Mother

Tongue Divine Science: Writings on the Mystical Philosophy of Margherita Porete] (Naples: M. D'Auria, 1995); and *Le amiche di Dio: Scritti di mistica femminile* [*God's Women Friends: Writings by Female Mystics*] (Naples: M. D'Auria, 2001).

    6. Bono and Kemp, "Introduction" to *Italian Feminist Thought*, op. cit., p. 9.

    7. Lonzi, "Let's Spit on Hegel," in Bono and Kemp, op. cit., pp. 40–42. See Muraro, "The Narrow Door," trans. Julia Hairston, in Laura Benedetti, Julia Hairston, and Silvia Ross, eds., *Gendered Contexts: New Perspectives in Italian Cultural Studies* (New York: Peter Lang, 1996), pp. 7–17, and "The Passion of Feminine Difference Beyond Equality," trans. Carmen di Cinque, in Graziella Parati and Rebecca West, eds., *Italian Feminist Theory and Practice: Equality and Sexual Difference* (Madison: Fairleigh Dickinson University Press, 2002), pp. 77–87.

    8. See for example *In Spite of Plato: A Feminist Rewriting of Ancient Philosophy*, trans. Serena Anderlini-D'Onofrio and Áine O'Healy (New York: Routledge, 1995). Cavarero is perhaps the most regularly translated figure in Italian feminist philosophy.

    9. See Muraro, "The Narrow Door," op. cit., pp. 11–13.

    10. Lucia Re examines both accusations in "Diotima's Dilemmas: Authorship, Authority, Authoritarianism," in Parati and West, op. cit., pp. 50–74.

    11. See Negri, "The Italian Difference," trans. Lorenzo Chiesa, in Lorenzo Chiesa and Alberto Toscano, eds., *The Italian Difference: Between Nihilism and Biopolitics* (Melbourne: re.press, 2009), pp. 13–23; this volume also includes Muraro's essay "The Symbolic Independence from Power," trans. Alberto Toscano, pp. 81–94. These features of Muraro's thought find parallels in Negri's own, and they account in part for his enthusiasm: female separatism echoes the logic of exodus from capitalist relations of domination; the distinction between female "authority" and male "power" resembles the distinction between constituent power [*potenza*] and constituted Power [*potere*]; last, the preference for strong metaphysical affirmations constitutes the point of closest resemblance between the two, in my view.

    12. Negri, op. cit., pp. 18–19. Andrea Righi offers a more concrete account of the relevance of Muraro's work for contemporary politics both within and beyond the feminist movement in "Origin and Dismeasure: The Thought of Sexual Difference in Luisa Muraro and Ida Dominijanni, and the Rise of Post-Fordist Psychopathology," in *Res Publica: Revista di Filosofía Política* 29 (2013), pp. 35–56.

Author's Note to the English-Language Edition

C'è chi ha pensato che valga la pena di far conoscere le idee espresse in questo libro, *L'ordine simbolico della madre*, anche a donne e uomini di lingua inglese. Bene.

Il libro è apparso a Roma, presso gli Editori Riuniti, nel 1991. Sono passati parecchi anni, a differenza delle altre traduzioni. Leggendolo nella versione inglese, ho sentito l'esigenza di togliere alcuni passi, di modificarne altri e di fare qualche aggiunta. Ho inteso così alleggerire il testo da frasi divenute insignificanti o superflue, e per un altro verso renderlo più comprensibile.

Ma i miei interventi, come ora riconosco, hanno anche un altro motivo, quasi un significato magico. Ho accettato, ma non ho mai cercato di essere tradotta in inglese. Il mio italiano mi sembra intraducibile in inglese, specialmente a causa della sintassi. Nella sintassi del mio italiano io ho espresso dei movimenti di pensiero che quella inglese non può fare suoi. Vero? Falso? Non sono in grado di giudicare. I miei interventi sulla versione inglese—ecco il significato magico—accompagnano il libro nel suo viaggio così come la moglie metteva la foto del matrimonio nella valigia del marito emigrante. (*L.M.*)

There are people who think that it is worthwhile to make the ideas expressed in this book, *The Symbolic Order of the Mother*, known to English-speaking women, and men, too.

Well, the book was published in Rome in 1991 by Editori Riuniti. Unlike other books and their translations, many years have passed between the publication of my book and the publication of its translation. While reading the English version of the book, I felt the need to delete some passages, modify others, and make some additions. I did so in order to relieve the text of sentences that have become unimportant or superfluous, and also to make the text easier to understand.

However, I recognize now that my interventions also have another motive, almost a magical meaning. I have accepted but never sought to be translated into English. I feel that my Italian is untranslatable into English, especially because of its syntax. In the syntax of my Italian, I expressed some movements of thought that the English language cannot make its own. True? False? I am not in a position to judge. My interventions in the English version—and here is the magical meaning—accompany the book in its journey just like a wife used to put her wedding photo into the suitcase of her emigrating husband. (*L.M.*)

Preface

This book describes a personal search inspired by a concept—the symbolic order of the mother—developed through the collaborative thinking of women with whom I have been doing politics and philosophy for many years: the women of the Milan Women's Bookstore and the philosophical community Diotima, at the University of Verona.

Writing this book has taken me twelve months, four of which were spent searching for the starting point. Once I found it, I wrote step by step as thoughts came to my mind, at first with difficulty and then impetuously, interrupted every now and then by new difficulties.

In the course of this work I have been helped and at times guided by Piera Bosotti. Without her intelligent reading I would not always have known where I was going. I thank her heartily.

The notes do not mirror the progress of my search, because they were all written at the end. According to my custom, they contain bibliographic information, comments, and also additions and corrections to the main text. I hope I have not written a useless book; writing it was certainly not that for me.

March 10, 1991

CHAPTER 1

The Difficulty of Beginning

I wanted to write on a theme about which I felt I had something to say and felt like saying it. But I was not able to begin.

If I have to go some distant place, like New York or Palermo, I hesitate a little before making up my mind, even if the place attracts me. Once I resolve to go, however, I manage to leave and get there without difficulty. As a matter of fact, once the decision is made, things arrange themselves, and I know what I have to do. I can easily tell what depends on me, what I must take into consideration, and what I can disregard. And from beginning to end I act accordingly.

On the other hand, although my experience of writing is no less extensive than my experience of travel, the decision to write does not have the same effect on my thoughts. Rather, it has almost the opposite effect of putting my thoughts into disorder. Consequently, I find myself torn among different choices, uncertain about what can be done. I easily fall prey to the most unpredictable second thoughts, and many times I find myself compelled to start again and to go ahead with a thousand uncertainties.

This writing would have not been any different, except that this time the starting point became, after many second thoughts, interrogating the difficulty of starting at all and bringing to an end an undertaking made of words.

My dream was always to make of this undertaking something perfectly logical, that is, something provided with a perfect correspondence among me, the language I use, and what I said. If I could do this, I thought, my words would support themselves from within, through the force of the order they express, without interference from anything else. I thought that, little by little, as I got closer to this coherence I would contend less and less with my doubts and second thoughts, because the words would show that they do not depend on me, although I have written them. They would have been written as if they were dictated to me because of the correspondence between what I wrote and what demanded to be written, which would be so close and visible. In this correspondence, I would be as tranquil as a queen on her throne.

I turned to philosophy. Although philosophy seemed to be made to help me, it did not. Quite the reverse—in the long run, I discovered later, it trapped my mind.

This discovery came at two different moments. The first moment came when I was studying philosophy at school. There I learned, among other things, the importance of the starting point. If I were to say not just anything, but that which demands to be said by me, I would be able to proceed logically. The beginning of a work that has the quality of being logical would naturally be so in its turn. That is, the beginning would be logical not only in fact but also in principle, so that nothing essential would be presupposed by it, and everything would have to follow the logic of the beginning without being forced. Finding a logical beginning is as important as it is difficult. According to Hegel "the difficulty of beginning" is a specialty of philosophy.[1] In philosophy, "the principle ought also to be the beginning, and what is the first for thought ought also to be the first in the *process* of thinking."[2] The beginning in philosophy is like its seed, in the sense that philosophy develops from within itself. Another metaphor used for philosophical undertaking, besides the botanical one, is the engineering metaphor of foundations. Both metaphors give the idea of something that stands by itself, which is what I was looking for.

When I came to see how philosophers solve the problem of beginning in a logical manner, I noticed that all of them try, in a variety of ways, to simplify the starting point to the utmost by eliminating from it much, as much as possible, of what can actually be found there the moment one begins to do philosophy. None of them begins from the given reality, as I would have done. The argument they often give is that the beginning, if it is logical, is also the foundation, and as such it cannot contain anything that could reveal itself to be false, transient, or deceptive, which could invalidate the construction.

A great philosopher of the beginning as a foundation is Descartes. His way of reasoning is typical because he excludes from the starting point knowledge gained through the senses, even though up to that time, such knowledge was considered the most certain. In the first of the *Meditations on First Philosophy* he writes: "I have found that the senses deceive, and it is prudent never to trust completely those who have deceived us even once."[3] Therefore, Descartes excludes not only deception, which is obvious, but also the possibility of its occurrence, even when this occurrence is also the occurrence of the true, as in the case of the senses. Would this not be an even worse deception?

Like Descartes, Locke also resorts to the metaphor of the foundation. As is well known, at the basis of all knowledge Locke puts experience reduced to sensation (of external material things) plus reflection (on the processes of our mind): there is nothing else, neither father, nor mother, nor language, nor needs, nor feelings . . . Usually this excessive rigor is corrected later. For example, Descartes himself, whose foundation-beginning excludes feeling as an attribute of "thinking matter," later corrects himself and again takes feeling into consideration in order to assimilate it to a way of thinking. Then, at the beginning of the twentieth century, Husserl corrects the Cartesian abstract conception of thinking without having been thought (of feeling without having been felt, etc.). But the tendency to make the beginning an absolute principle and to make the philosophical undertaking a type of construction was not corrected. Thus, Husserl says that to enter into philosophy we must rid ourselves of the "bond . . . of the pregivenness of the world."[4]

Philosophers arouse criticism in me that is perhaps justified but secondary. The blockage of the first phase of my research was due not so much to the simplifications of the philosophers as to the use I made of them. Perhaps I should tell what my reaction was when I learned that in order to philosophize we must bracket what we normally have before us. And in short, this necessity rather fascinated me. It seems to me that the whole history of Western philosophy transmits this fascination. It is like a promise of happy abduction, of elevation above all and everybody. This desire goes back to Plato and maybe, even earlier, to Parmenides.

Plato's excessive rigor regarding the beginning of philosophizing is the object of a powerful mise-en-scène that from ancient culture has filtered into Christian and modern culture, and even to us today.

I am referring to the strange symbolic "parable" of Book VII of *The Republic*, known as the myth of the cave.[5] As is well-known, in this myth the philosopher compares the human condition to the condition of men imprisoned in a deep cave with their faces turned toward its back. Into this cave come the shadows and echoes of a world unknown to them. One of the men is released and taken outside into the blinding daylight, to which he slowly grows accustomed until he can look at the sun.

Throughout the tale, there is no sign of desire: the prisoner is snatched away from his condition and forced out. Nor can we find manifestations of joy—only grief, difficulty, and discomfort. The character Socrates explains that "it is a question of . . . the turning about of the soul from a day that is like night to the veritable day" . . . "the conversion of the soul itself from the kingdom of generation to truth and being."[6]

In the *Discourse on Method*, Descartes's tale of his mental itinerary in the room with the majolica stove where he had the idea of the method can be read as a modern version of the myth of the cave. The myth has not been directly transposed and, although I cannot prove it, it seems to me that the myth has been passed down through medieval culture. At least this is the impression I had when I read the texts. The ascent of the prisoner from the depths of the cave corresponds to Descartes's theory of leaving childhood and its "appetites," leaving his homeland and the schoolbooks that had filled his mind with errors and doubts. After a period of travel and of various work experiences, he was convinced that he could not give credit even to what he learned by example and habit. So he resolved to study himself as if he were the only book that could teach him to tell the true from the false. On this foundation he planned to rebuild the whole body of the sciences. As for the reality of experience, he would regard it with a detachment less dramatic but no less radical than that of the prisoner who has emerged from the depths of the cave:

> I shall think that the sky, the air, the earth, colours, shapes, sounds and all external things are merely the delusions of dreams which he [the malicious demon] has devised to ensnare my judgement. I shall consider myself as not having hands or eyes, or flesh, or blood or senses, but as falsely believing that I have all these things.[7]

Husserl also describes the beginning of philosophizing with words that remind us of the fascinating beauty of Plato's text, for example, when he says that "we who are philosophizing in a new way" go through a period that he describes as a "*total change* of the natural attitude, such that we no longer live as heretofore." It is a period of "total transformation . . . which we resolve to take up once and for all," and it is like a "liberation."⁸

But this kind of philosophizing, the conception of philosophy to which I was attracted, was fruitless. I will relate an incident. I attended the University of Louvain. I could not decide whether to study logic or linguistics. I chose linguistics, and after some months of intense study I went to show the work I had done to a linguist. He seemed perplexed. I explained the general lines of my work, and he remarked: "You should begin from the most recent research; you will look at the beginning later, if necessary." I had done nothing but study Saussure with the idea that by going back to the beginning I should have understood [*capito*] the rest. Or, I should say, I would have known [*saputo*] the rest. I was disconcerted when I heard the linguist's words. They contradicted what I believed to be obvious, and they showed how my conviction was not obvious to all. I became even more disconcerted to see suddenly how correct his words were, although at the time I could hardly articulate this, and certainly my adviser did not suspect it. I realized that, roughly speaking, I began from the beginning because I was unable to start from where I was, and this was because I was nowhere.

I stuck with philosophy and with my conception of it. As often happens, what attracted me to philosophy and what stopped me from moving on in philosophy were basically the same thing. I was drawn to philosophy because I was looking for symbolic independence from given reality. I did not want to find myself mentally at the mercy of random and unexpected events any more. I was not able to get to that symbolic independence because I finally understood that philosophy, although it sheltered me from the whimsical domain of the real, set me against my mother, whose work I implicitly judged to be ill-made. I wanted to get to the beginning of things in order to understand and to understand myself, and to do so I went against my mother. This is not something that I explicitly thought or that was taught to me in philosophy, at least not in these terms. But this is what doing philosophy came to mean to me. Why on earth did I think of it in such terms? Because, unknown to me, there was inside of me an unacknowledged aversion toward the author of my life that philosophy came to reawaken. And because between philosophy and this unarticulated feeling, a vicious circle had developed. The more I looked for symbolic independence, the more the fear of given reality and subjection to it grew inside of me.

Probably my first inclination toward philosophy was not an innocent choice. Probably from the beginning I was moved by an unconscious will to invalidate the authority and the work of the mother. My philosophical preferences would confirm this. I chose philosophers and a conception of philosophy in transparent rivalry, at least in the language utilized, to all that belongs to the matrix of life. Just think of Plato and how he insistently opposes the search for being and truth to the "kingdom of generation."

However, I am sure that I did not turn to philosophy as a result of my aversion to the mother, although later both came together in the manner I am describing. I am sure of this for two different reasons. The first, simple reason is that my entrance into philosophy, or specifically my choice of studies, was authorized by my mother on my request. The second reason is that, once I found the way out of the trap, philosophy soon took on a new sense, favorable to the new direction of my research.

But I have found the way out with the politics of women and not with philosophy. From the politics of women I have learned that for her free existence, a woman needs the symbolic power of the mother in the same way that she needed her mother's physical power to come into the world. From the politics of women I have also learned that a woman can have the power of the mother completely on her side in an exchange of love and recognition. Before the politics of women there was neither love nor recognition between the power of the mother, on one hand, and my needs, on the other. (I could not pass in love and recognition between the power of the mother, on the one hand, and my needs, on the other.) Lacking that, I believed that my aspiration to the symbolic independence of philosophy was antithetical to what seemed to me the arbitrary, and not well defined, reign of the author of my life.

The vicious circle of which I spoke earlier closed right over this deformed image of the mother. I felt and acted as if the woman who brought me into the world was the enemy of my symbolic independence.

It was as if my symbolic independence necessarily involved my separation from her and from her purpose—a way of thinking common to many women. Actually it is not correct to call it a way of thinking; rather, it is something implied, it is almost a schema underlying a whole way of feeling and acting. For women, nothing from the outside comes to refute this state of affairs—as if it were natural that a woman should detest her mother and feel detested by her. In reality, it is a question of a terrible symbolic disorder.

Now, I ask myself, to what extent has philosophy perpetuated this disorder?

There is no doubt that both the history of philosophy and the culture of which it is part show signs of a rivalry with the work and the authority of the mother. Plato's symbolic tale, which shaped the *forma mentis* of the ancients as well as medieval and modern people, contains the evident metaphor of a second birth. And outside of this metaphor, which is not left to the reader's intuition but is, instead, explicitly delineated, there is a political conception of the just and the true that aims to supplant another symbolic order. Plato calls this other order the kingdom of generation and he presents it as intrinsically unjust and deceptive.

This operation will be repeated innumerable times. It is a very simple operation that can almost be confused with the operation of metaphor, the most common of the figures. It consists in transferring to cultural production (such as science, law, religion, etc.) the attributes of the power and the work of the mother, depriving and reducing the mother to an opaque and formless nature, above whom the knowing, ruling, believing subject must rise in order to dominate her. As Husserl says, "through the epoché a new way of experiencing, of thinking, of theorizing, is opened to the philosopher; here, situated *above* his own natural being and *above* the natural world, he loses nothing of their being and their objective truths and likewise nothing at all of the spiritual acquisitions of his world-life," and so on (Husserl's emphasis).[9]

As Luce Irigaray teaches, perhaps Freud's theory of parricide, derived from Sophocles's *Oedipus*, is not at the origin of our culture. Instead, as Euripides's *Oresteia* suggests, there is matricide. Irigaray writes that men have made of their sex a tool to dominate the power of the mother.

Philosophical language confirms this view. Between patriarchy and the development of philosophy there is a complicity that I did not take into account when I turned to it to find symbolic independence. Now I see that the kingdom of generation and the natural world of which philosophers speak are not nature—whether good or bad, ordered or chaotic, it matters little—but they are the possibility of another symbolic order that does not deprive the mother of her qualities. And I see that the cosmologies of the philosophers are also political treatises, perhaps even more so than the treatises explicitly dedicated to politics.

But there is the risk that I am committing against philosophy the wrong I have done to the mother, that of attributing to her the lack of what she cannot be and also the excess of what she can be in order to relieve myself of my own lacks and excesses. There is the risk that I am doomed to repeat this operation indefinitely. Because I lack a logical beginning, I go around in a circle and always start all over again without ever reaching symbolic independence.

It is true that the philosophy to which I turned in order to evade the blind authoritarianism of things (and of the mother, according to my mistaken notion) kept me in my mistake and consequently aggravated the mental disorder I was experiencing. But could not this effect be imputed to philosophy that has been improperly pursued rather than to philosophy itself? I myself admitted earlier that my inclination to philosophy was perhaps not pure. Maybe from the very beginning I had intended to invalidate the work and the authority of the mother.

Many philosophers have considered the possibility of making improper uses of philosophy. Plato discourages the teaching of dialectics to those who, because of youth or disposition, "treat argument as a form of sport solely for the purposes of contradiction" in imitation of the true philosophers, so that they end up "rush[ing] to the conclusion that all they once believed is false."[10] Could not this be my case? Shortly after this passage Plato specifies that women are not excluded from political office and consequently from the philosophical education that is indispensable to those who rule.[11] And as he did in regard to men, Plato adds about these women that they are "women who are found to have the necessary gifts."[12]

If a woman does not have the necessary gifts, she could turn to philosophy for reasons that true philosophers do not have, such as, for instance, in order to compete with the mother and supplant her. This would explain why such a woman would not succeed in benefiting from philosophy in her search for a way to think and live logically.

If I look at the works of great philosophers, I almost think that the problem can be reduced to the bad use of philosophy by people (e.g., women) who are not gifted for it. Those philosophers speak in a beautiful manner. They immerse themselves in the deep waters of doubt (Descartes's image) without drowning in them, and they emerge regenerated a few pages later (in Descartes's case—it takes longer for others). They plan and carry out huge and radical deconstructions from which nothing is spared. And, nonetheless, these philosophers are always greatly supported by their language. They choose and reject with unfailing criteria among the givens of their historical context. They separate themselves from given reality without losing contact with it, just as they also separate themselves from tradition but not from what nurtures it (for this point I have in mind especially the relationship between Christian and Greek philosophers). And in all of this they are apparently untouched by the ghosts of retaliation against maternal power. I charge them with having silenced that power, after having imitated it and stripped it away.

As a matter of fact, in the use of language as well as in relation to present reality and to earlier thinking, these men show a capacity for symbolic weaving that I have lacked (I think again of the incident in Louvain) and that I now know they must have learned from their familiarity with the matrix of life. They show they have frequently come in contact with it and have learned its art.

But this is not what they teach. Philosophers do not teach and, perhaps, are not able to teach how to weave symbolically, an ability they learned in their relationship with the mother. This ability has come to them thanks to a historical privilege that they seem to believe is a gift fallen from the sky or their natural attribute. The patriarchal society in which philosophy has developed regards the love between mother and son as its most precious good. This love is the hearth where great desires glow; it is the kitchen of sublime undertakings, the workshop of the law. Everything seems to link up with it. If there is one thing I envy about men—and how could I not envy it—it is the culture of the mother's love in which they are brought up. This is the practical foundation; this is the living seed from which philosophical discourse develops.

But philosophers do not give any account of this. Ignoring the historical privilege of sons, they mask with ideal foundations the origin of their knowledge. They love a silent mother whose work they present as an image and an approximation of their own, and by doing so they overthrow the order of things.

On the other hand, if I do not have the necessary gifts for philosophy, this must also be seen neither as a misfortune willed by heaven nor a fault of nature. Rather, it is a historical condition. I was born into a culture that does not teach women to love the mother. Yet it is the most important knowledge; without it, it is difficult to learn the rest and be original in something . . .

Suddenly I realize that the beginning I have been looking for is in front of me: it is knowing how to love [*il saper amare*] the mother. That this is so is certain because other beginnings are not possible for me. As a matter of fact, only this beginning breaks the vicious circle and frees me from the trap of a culture that, by not teaching me to love my mother, has also deprived me of the strength required to change it, leaving me only with indefinite laments.

But how will I learn? Who will teach me? The answer is simple: I will learn from my necessity, which is so great and so skillful that it has already taught me what it means to love the mother. I discover that this necessity has always been with me, and it has always supported me in my search for the order that will give me symbolic independence. As a matter of fact, what else was this ever-greater difficulty of beginning if not an incentive to induce me to keep looking until I could find the true beginning? In the end, this was also a way to make me get to the starting point. Even that obscure feeling of aversion I carried inside of me, which became stronger with the failed attempts to reach symbolic independence, was a way of finding the beginning.

According to Freud, the initial love or attachment, as he calls it, of the little girl for her mother is very strong, but it is almost always destined to turn into hatred. He says that the existence of that love is clear, but it does not last because the daughter must detach herself from the mother, and "the turning away from the mother is accompanied by hostility; the attachment to the mother ends in hate."[13] In the past, when I read those statements, I sometimes considered them false and misogynous and other times sadly true. But their truth is the result of patriarchy. Now I consider those assertions superficial. In reality, there is no transformation of love into hatred, but only the inability to love, so that the initial attachment goes wrong and it becomes like a wound that does not heal.

In this way, then, the difficulty of beginning was solved, and I have found the logical beginning for my research. It is a poorer beginning than the most severe of the philosophies of foundation-beginning would require. As a matter of fact, my knowledge of how to love the mother is anything but rich. It includes a few items of substance won by a perhaps rather long and compelling but almost unconscious negotiation [*contrattazione*]. It is a negotiation that I have carried out so far only because I was caught between attachment and aversion, aversion and fear of retaliation.

But I have found the beginning, and I can already say: it is only the beginning! Therefore, I feel rich and I move on. Philosophers disagree with each other on the limits of knowledge and power. I put myself among those who do not admit absolute limits. As a matter of fact, I do not see a limit to what I can obtain from a mother who has freely given me my life. In the same way, there will be no more limits to my demands, now that I have learned to formulate them.

Chapter Notes

Chapter 1, page 1: What would I have liked to write that I did not manage to begin writing? I do not know what it was because that never took shape; maybe it is exactly what, in the end, I am writing here. What I know instead is the theme: the politics of women. I began writing the very moment I realized how philosophy had trapped me by promising to teach me how to undertake a perfectly logical enterprise that resonated with the antimaternal feelings in me. However, I have not abandoned the idea of undertaking a perfectly logical enterprise. What I mean is that I did not find the starting point by renouncing that enterprise, but by making it agree, instead of competing, with that love that bound me from an early age to the woman who gave me life.

Chapter 1, pages 1–2: I cannot say what I mean exactly by logical and logic. Maybe I will know that later. In a philosophical work such uncertainty might seem a bit shameful. However, I think it is justified. If I am not sure, rather than give a wrong definition of something that in its name and in history requires rigor, I had better not give any. That's it, what I have just said is logical enough.

Chapter 1, page 6: I call the mother the author of life. And the father? The question will be raised when patriarchy begins to decline. Perhaps that is right now. If we give credit to the child's point of view—as I think we should in these things—the father is in the first place the companion of the mother; the man she chose or accepted for company and work; second, and thanks to her words, he will later be recognized as coauthor.

Chapter 1, page 7: From the very beginning in philosophy I searched, unaware and unsuccessfully, for a solution to my symbolic disorder. The purpose of my search was to achieve symbolic independence, which approximately meant being able to say *I* even when I am, materially, a *we* or an impersonal entity (for instance, in the hands of a nurse on duty). The relationship between not knowing how to love the mother and the symbolic disorder is intuitive. It is not difficult to intuit how completely we are exposed to the arbitrary domination of others and of things when we do not know how to love the mother. Women's body against body in relation to the real is manifested in their notorious tendency to fantasize about love and in a less well-known underhand resistance to doing what they are supposed to do. In her *Notebooks*, Simone Weil writes about her enigmatic inability to carry out small tasks such as cleaning her room, a task she imposed on herself. To me, typical female virtues of diligence and docility hide the substantial lack of corresponding human qualities. This phenomenon has given me a useful hint for my research. I believe that fantasizing about love, a true hemorrhage of female energies, and also women's rebellion against the order of necessity (which in its turn wastes incalculable energies) can be traced back to the fact that we do not know how to love the mother. In reference to women's conflict with the real, I use the expression "body against body in relation to reality" from the title of a conference organized by Luce Irigaray, "Body against Body in Relation to the Mother"—a concept she explains in her article with that title published in *Sexes and Genealogies*, trans. Gillian C. Gill (New York: Columbia University Press, 1993), 9–21.

Chapter 1, page 7: In the same conference, "Body against Body in Relation to the Mother," Irigaray proposes that matricide is the origin of our social order. "Orestes kills his mother because the empire of God-Father, who has seized and taken for his own the ancient powers . . . of the earth-mother, demands it" (12). Further on Irigaray writes, "man, and the race of men, has transformed the male organ into an instrument of power with which to master maternal power . . ." (17).

Chapter 1, pages 8: Twice I interrupt my critique of ancient and modern classical philosophy to say: "perhaps it is a justified critique but surely it is secondary." I could say the same thing of the critique of classical philosophy by contemporary thought, known as critical theory, weak and postmodern thought, and so on represented by thinkers such as Derrida, Foucault, and Vattimo. The critique of logocentrism (which in feminism becomes a critique of logophallocentrism) may be justified but it is secondary if it is done from the point of view of a logo-eccentric experience, such as mine, because of its symbolic disorder. If the focus of my research were the critique of Western philosophy I would end up protracting my symbolic disorder. For me, it is enough to unlearn what I have never been able to learn.

Chapter 1, page 10: Before Freud, the Marquis de Sade relates the hatred of the daughter for the mother to women's sexual liberation. In the fifth dialogue of *Philosophy in the Bedroom* Sade writes, "I want the law to allow women to give themselves to as many men as they please; I want women to be allowed to enjoy all sexes and all parts of the body, just as men do." In the seventh and last dialogue, the young Eugenie, who has been taught sexual pleasures by a group of libertines, hurls herself at her mother who has come to take her back home:

> MADAME DE MISTIVAL: Oh merciful heaven! my Eugenie is doomed, 'tis evident . . . Eugenie, my beloved Eugenie, for the last time heed the supplications of her who gave you your life; these are orders no longer, but prayers; unhappily, it is only too true that you are amidst monsters here; tear yourself from this perilous commerce and follow me; I ask it of you on my knees! (*She falls to her knees*)
>
> DOLMANCE: Ah, very pretty! a tearful scene! . . . To it, Eugenie! Be tender.
>
> EUGENIE, *half-naked, as the reader surely must remember:* Here you are, my dear little Mamma, I bring you my buttocks . . . There they are, positively at the level of your lips; kiss them, my sweet, suck them, 'tis all Eugenie can do for you . . . Remember, Dolmance: I shall always show myself worthy of having been your pupil.

The scene rises to a crescendo of Eugenie's fantasized violence toward poor Madame de Mistival (from Marquis de Sade, *Philosophy in the Bedroom*, trans. Richard Seaver and Austryn Wainhouse [New York: Grove Press, 1966], 270 and 355–56). Of course, Freud's language is rather different from Sade's. "We will now turn our interest on to the single question of what it is that brings this powerful attachment of the girl to her mother to an end. This, as we know, is its usual fate: it is destined to make room for an attachment to her father. Here we come upon a fact that is a pointer to our further advance. This step in development does not involve only a simple change of object. The turning away from the mother is accompanied by hostility; the attachment to the mother ends in hate. A hate of that kind may become very striking and last all through life; it may be carefully overcompensated later on; as a rule one part of it is overcome while another part persists." Sigmund Freud, *The Standard Edition of the Complete Psychological Works of Sigmund Freud*, trans. James Strachey 24 vols. (London: Hogarth Press, 1932–36), vol. 22, 121–22. Although they use different language, the Marquis de Sade and Freud both draw a parallel between the daughter-mother relationship and that of the son-father as a necessary rebellion and a symbolic killing. Both of them also conceive female sexuality according to the model of male sexuality. The man is the paradigm for the woman. This is so according to the modern conception of equality between men and women, a concept that does not include the thought of sexual difference. This explains how equality as it is being codified in our culture is an apparatus of impositions forced on women who have no alternatives except that of going back to their traditional subordination, and how such a form of equality is at the same time the origin of inequality, caught in a vicious circle.

Chapter 1, page 10: Now I want to return to symbolic independence. There is symbolic independence if there is symbolic order. Our concept of symbolic order (which is perhaps the major product of the philosophical work of our century) originates, according to my reading (which does not rule out other readings), in the failure of Wittgenstein's *Tractatus Logico-Philosophicus*. Frankly speaking, this book is rather odd because it formulates a theory of language based, on the one hand, on a debatable interpretation of Russell's logic and, on the other hand, on ignorance of the most elementary science and philosophy of language. However, thanks to this book, a whole line of scientific and philosophic research of a positivist nature was pushed to the point of failure because the book showed how, in this type of research, the sayable can say *everything* except what interests us. I quote one of the last statements in Wittgenstein's work, proposition 6.52: "We feel that even if *all possible* scientific questions be answered, the problems of life have still not been touched at all. Of course there is then no question left, and just this is the answer," *Tractatus Logico-Philosophicus* (London: Routledge, 1922), 187. The concept of symbolic order and its determining importance came into my life and into my text when I discovered what I call its logical beginning; that is, knowing how to love the mother. What difference do I see between logical and symbolic order? Almost none, but at the same time I see a huge difference. For instance, the difference I see is that the symbolic order in order to be such depends on our acceptance of it. This means that the symbolic order is historical and that it can be changed. It also explains why it is propagandized and imposed on us, for instance through education. When the symbolic order is imposed on us it is clear that it is not an order anymore but a disorder, which manifests itself in many ways such as personality problems and the loss of intelligence, which should be seen not as psychological problems but as consequences of symbolic disorder, as Freud and psychoanalysis understood.

Then there is the social order based on relationships of force, which remains an order even when it is imposed on us. The three orders (or, if we prefer, the three ordering instances of human reality) always operate together but sometimes in harmony, sometimes in conflict, sometimes in confusion, weakening one another. The symbolic instance is not the strongest, but for me it is the most important because freedom is its principle. This freedom is not in logic or in society, whereas through reasoning and social action we actually express our freedom and nonfreedom. The symbolic order regulating us by making us feel free is first of all the language we speak. Our symbolic disorder too manifests itself in the most precise way in the language we speak.

Chapter 1, page 11: Concerning the limits of knowledge and power, I include myself among those who do not admit absolute limits. I'd like to make this note: the sense of limit is that we establish it in order to overcome it. As a matter of fact, once the limit is established, it is already potentially overcome. Nowadays, there is a sort of feminine public teaching (for instance, about science after the very serious incident at the atomic base in Chernobyl, in the Ukraine, USSR) that is not accompanied by any attempt to overcome it. I am afraid that this goes against women's search for freedom in that within the patriarchal social order women are seen (and see themselves) as bearers of an absolute limit. The lack of expression of female desire results in what men call castration, which appears to me to be evident in some feminist philosophy of science.

CHAPTER 2

Knowing How to Love the Mother as a Sense of Being

In just the time it takes to turn the page, I have already become less poor, much less poor. I will explain how. For years I have been nourished on philosophy, good philosophy as it is generally judged from a viewpoint that was not my own. From my point of view, instead, it was only a philosophy I learned badly, uselessly, and with difficulty. I was aware of this and I used to say it to those who taught me philosophy. For instance, I used to say that philosophy is dead, and so forth. I used to say, "It is dead" to try to explain the feeling of fatigue and pointlessness in my philosophical work, which the school, in fact, considered good (though not very good, to be fair).

Now what has happened is that knowing how to love the mother—to learn more of which remains a strong desire within me—is giving philosophy back to me by turning it to my good. From the viewpoint of content, not all of it is good. I can see clearly enough that a great portion of philosophical thought is shoddy, as I can also see that not all of it is bad, and that all I have learned can be useful to me.

This entirely contradicts a very typical feminist idea, which I share and perhaps also support. The idea is that we women have been invaded and colonized by a male culture and consequently we must rid ourselves of it through a process that will inevitably be long, full of struggle and pain . . . just like the prisoner who comes out of Plato's cave!

But in reality, this is not how it goes. The moment I found this clue and grasped that logic required that I learn to love the mother, what I learned earlier turns out to be useful to me. I do not have to make an effort to peel off ways of being and thinking infused by patriarchal culture, although I developed within it. How can I explain the astonishing lightness I now feel? How can I explain my happiness at having my past of painful philosophical work restored to me? (To be clear, I do not rule out that later there may be new fatigues and new pains. Philosophical work in itself is neither light nor gratuitous. Here I refer only to my relationship with the work I have already done in the past, work that I thought had to be undone because of its ambiguous, antimaternal meaning.)

The explanation I found is that although there are surely antimaternal contents in my philosophical culture, I could not entirely absorb them for the simple reason that the very antimaternal meaning of much philosophy has prevented me from learning it well. In other words, suppose that the most rigorous feminism is right about the necessity to unlearn patriarchal culture, and I agree with that, my problem turns out to be very simple because to me it is a question of unlearning what I have never been able to learn. On the other hand, what I have learned turns out to be useful to me, as if my mother herself had taught me.

I tend to think that everything I have learned well was somehow taught to me by my mother herself. I cannot say how she taught me, but I mean what I say literally and not just in a manner of speaking.

I do not speak of the mother metaphorically. I speak of her realistically, and in order to be clear, I will renounce, as much as possible, the beautiful and rich language that develops from the metaphor of the mother and from the symbolism of birth. The symbolism of birth is present in various spheres, from the religious ceremony of baptism to artistic production, or to the conception (*conceptus*) of philosophy. These metaphors are commonly considered an acknowledgment [*riconoscimento*] of the magnitude of the work of the mother. But since this acknowledgment too often does not recognize the social authority of women in the flesh, I think that it is rather a way of depriving the mother of her prerogatives.

In fact, the metaphors and symbols of the mother imply and sustain the parallelism between natural life and culture together with an unlimited series of oppositions and analogies between one and the other. In this way, they cover up other kinds of relationships such as disparities, irreversibilities, dependencies, and all the other possible mixtures. The consequence of this is to rule out of bounds what mothers actually do that is absolute and not appropriable, starting from the fact that mothers, besides doing what the registry office calls them mothers for, also teach their children to speak and do many other things that are foundations of human civilization. Mothers do all of this concurrently, and not in parallel or, least of all, by analogy.

Therefore, I also refuse to represent my coming to consciousness [*presa di coscienza*] as a second birth, although I find this image in Adrienne Rich ("I am a woman giving birth to myself") and in Luce Irigaray ("This return to the world is also necessary for women"), two authors whose thought, by the way, helps me greatly in this research.[1] The idea of bringing oneself into the world again, to the extent that it is in agreement with a culture that makes a metaphor of generation (perhaps there is a different way of expressing this), makes us believe that we can make the work of our mother reversible or superfluous. I must add that this severe precaution against metaphors imposes itself on me and on women like me, and not on all women in general. It imposes itself against the backdrop of a difficulty in having a relationship of recognition [*rapporto riconoscente*] with the woman who has brought us into the world. It imposes itself on those women who want to learn how to love the mother.

I do not speak of the mother metaphorically. I speak of her symbolically. Many confuse the symbolic with the metaphorical. To make the difference clear, let us think of bread for starving people or of drugs for addicts. For them bread or drugs are associated with everything, and so it takes on an enormous meaning. But it is not a metaphorical meaning that prevails in the language of others, that is, of the well-fed and of those who are not drug addicts.

I will write what the mother means to me. But first I must say that the discovery of the nonmetaphoric symbolicity of the mother has not been waiting for discovery by me in order to take place. As a matter of fact, the nonmetaphoric symbolicity of the mother already has a place, and it is a very strong place, a fortress in our childhood. During childhood, we worshiped the mother and all that is related to her, from the husband she had to the shoes she wore, from the sound of her voice to the smell of her skin. We have put her at the center of a magnificent and realistic mythology. I entrust to the little girl I was, to those little girls with whom I grew up, to the little girls and boys who live among us, I entrust to them the task of testifying to the nonmetaphorical symbolicity of the mother. I take up the secondary task of translating this into philosophy.

This formula summarizes the sense of my writing clearly, but it is incomplete. I am introducing into philosophy what my mother means to me on the basis of what she meant when I needed her and depended on her totally. I must add that I was introduced to philosophy, as with everything else I know, by my mother. As I have already written, I do not know how it happened that she introduced me to philosophy, but that must be taken literally, and not metaphorically as philosophers do.

As we know, philosophers have drawn their inspiration from the figure and the work of the mother. They have presented the work of the mother as a copy (often a bad copy) of their own work by inverting the order of the work done. Because of that, philosophers have been complicit with patriarchy, which presents the father as the true author of life.[2]

Now I am less interested in criticizing than I am in affirming [*affermare*]. Once I understood the causes of my past incapacity to learn from philosophy how to think logically, and once I found that knowing how to love the mother was for me the principle of a logical order, I realized that criticizing per se does not lead anywhere. Criticizing is useful, and even necessary, but only if it comes after an affirmation that gives it purpose and measure.

I affirm that knowing how to love the mother creates symbolic order. As I see it, this is the implicit, although less and less implicit, affirmation, measure, and purpose of the women's movement that began at the end of the seventies.

Feminism has produced a profound critique of patriarchy and of the many philosophical, religious, literary, and other complicities supporting its system of dominion. But this massive and accurate labor of critique will be effaced in two or three generations if it does not find its affirmation. Only this affirmation can give back to society, and first of all to women, the symbolic power contained in the female relationship with the mother, which is neutralized by male domination.[3]

From the critique of patriarchy, I have learned consciousness-raising [*autocoscienza*] but not the capacity to freely give meaning to female grandeur, like that of my mother which I experienced and fully recognized in the first months and years of my life, and later on sadly lost and almost repudiated.

We have been taught that the negation of a negation makes an affirmation. This is not true in all conditions. There are cases in which the second negation confirms the first instead of eliminating it. It happened in my case. As a matter of fact, in my work of critique I was only carrying out a rejection of the sustenance of others' thought, and in doing so I indirectly made the mental turn of my unnoticed aversion for the mother worse. This happened because I did not have any other symbolic independence except that of my unconscious impulse to reject, and because in my body-against-body relation with maternal power, I was not culturally supported. Consequently, once I was engaged in the *Destruktion* characterizing the work of critique, I did not know how to stop.

In my eyes, Kant is a good philosophical example of the male readiness to stop himself in the process of destruction. Concerning Kant, school manuals explain that Kantian critique cannot be undertaken following the obvious meaning of the word, which is negative. Instead, it must be undertaken positively, as inquiry into the conditions that make positive scientific knowledge possible. Kant maintains this, too. But no science would be possible under the conditions he posits because of the lack of necessary energy. After having shown that metaphysics as a science is not possible, because it is not possible to know either the true reality of anything or the true existence of anyone, Kant shows his true positivity when he breaks off to praise metaphysics.

In the *Prolegomena* the halt imposed on intellectual critique shapes the text of a paragraph that would fit into a novel with a surprise ending [*romanza a sorpresa*]. Kant starts §57 by saying that, after having given evident proofs, it would be a great mistake to hope that one can know or claim that they can obtain even the slightest knowledge, and so on . . . How could we, in fact, determine the nature of reality in itself, and so forth? But—and it is at this point that the sudden halt occurs—it would be an even greater mistake to deny the reality of things in themselves. Because if it is true that we cannot form a definite concept of what things in themselves are, nonetheless, we cannot free ourselves from the need to refer to them either. And this leads, therefore, to Kant's conclusion that we must think an immaterial essence, an intelligible world and a Supreme Being, which are *noumena*, because only in them, as in things in themselves, does reason finds its completion and satisfaction.[4]

In the *Critique of Pure Reason*, Kant himself pointed out the logic he followed by pausing to discuss what he had critically demonstrated to be unknowable. He writes, "we are not satisfied with the exposition merely of that which is true, but likewise demand that account be taken of that which *we desire to know*" (my emphasis).[5] We state what we desire to know by putting that desire for knowledge out of the reach of critique. Although this operation is weak on the speculative level, it has been of great symbolic influence, as its developments show (I am thinking of Hegel, on the one hand, and of Schopenhauer, on the other). I believe that the influence of that operation is due to its ability to stop the series of negations that do not produce affirmation. This makes room for the affirmation of being that in Kant, as in much modern culture, speaks in the form of the desire to know.

I did not follow this path in my search to find once again the symbolic power of the relationship with the mother. Knowing how to love is a different path from the desire to know. It is almost the opposite because the desire to know directs the forces of the passions toward the objective of knowledge, which is, at any rate, stated to be unattainable. On the contrary, knowing how to love means putting the forces of the passions into circulation with the activity of the mind.

At this point I want to emphasize an even more circumscribed aspect to be found among great philosophers. This is their ability not entirely to trust intellectual labor and, instead, to know how to listen to the originary positivity of being, acknowledging that its being is stronger than intellectual mediation. I link this ability to the power of the mother. It is the aim of philosophers not to grant it to her. The Kantian thing-in-itself is the cenotaph of the mother, her empty tomb. By getting close to the power of the mother, philosophers learn the limit of intellectual labor. It is precisely the ability to go beyond the limits of the regime of mediation in force that makes a great thinker.

As I have said, I did not have this ability, and this made my critical work endless. Critique was my prevailing philosophical practice. Generally, after the first impulse passed, I did not enjoy doing critique. I considered it necessary, and I expected from it positive results that never came.

I did not subject everything to critique either. In fact, I saved from my critique those texts and authors, promoters or followers, of a certain course of ideas, such as Ferdinand de Saussure, whom I mentioned earlier in relation to the linguistics of our century. My other philosophical practice consisted of going back to the origins, and since I did not have a symbolic collocation, consequently I was not able to exchange ideas with others. Going back to the presumed sources made me believe that I could inform myself about everything. Obviously, nothing like that happened, but studying the supposedly originary authors gave me great pleasure, the reason for which I understand only now. It was a fantastic return to being taught by my mother.

Feminist critique was not enough to correct my mental disorder because it conformed too much to the inadequate logic of the negation of the negation. This logic let me believe that by overturning the order of generation I could bring myself into the world again and give life to my mother. Feminism attributed our mothers' miseries to patriarchal dominion. In this way it authorized us to dwell on those miseries. Consequently, in terms of the symbolic order, feminism did not do anything different from what patriarchy does.

I find the highest point of the feminist critique of patriarchy in Adrienne Rich's lines from the mid-seventies on her relationship with her mother. "I no longer have fantasies—they are the unhealed child's fantasies, I think—of some infinitely healing conversation with her, in which we could show all our wounds, transcend the pain we have shared as mother and daughter, say everything at last. But in writing these pages, I am admitting, at least, how important her existence is and has been for me."[6]

It is too little. We must not forget the childhood dream that contains the seed of a female culture of the mother's love. After all, it appears again in Rich's text itself where she talks about the need we have for the power of the mother, which is no different from that of our childhood. Rich remarks: "The cry of that female child in us need not be shameful or regressive; it is the germ of our desire to create a world in which strong mothers and strong daughters will be a matter of course."[7]

Desire once again. This is not surprising because only desire has the power to oppose intellectual constructions. In my case desire impelled me to halt a series of negations which did not lead to any affirmation. But desire used to come to me at repeated intervals accompanied by pain and did not open new doors. Desire by itself does not make symbolic order, but knowing how to love the mother creates this order (which I have defined as the act of making desire and mind circulate together). This order has made me completely overcome intellectualistic logic. Before, I swung indecisively between desire and intellectual labor.

Knowing how to love the mother has given me, or restored to me, an authentic sense of being of which I must now speak at length.[8]

By now it is obvious, I think, that I am not here to state something factually true, whether psychological or sociological or historical, concerning the relationships of women with the figure of the mother. That is, I am not here to state something true based on the correspondence between what is said to be and what proves to be, according to the classic definition of truth, which asserts that "the snow is white" if and only if the snow is white.

Many things I say have this type of correspondence-truth. As such they can be appropriately verified. But not everything, and not everything I say, can find verification. As a whole, what I am saying seeks to make sayable something that, otherwise, would not manage to be. In these cases, sense and being correspond because of the necessity of their appearing together. That is to say, if something is false, it is not even understood. Conversely, if something makes sense, it is also true.

To understand this point is to understand what metaphysics is. Philosophy, as I practice it today, works as the bridge between "physics," the realm of correspondence-truth, and metaphysics, where truth reigns as a sense of being. (In the past, and even today, many prejudices about metaphysics have arisen from confusing the two realms and from regarding metaphysics on a par with a "physics" and its rule of correspondence-truth.) To give an example, let us consider Freud's *metapsychology*. The term was coined from the term *metaphysics*, and this is intentional since, in the writings under that title, Freud does not put himself in the position of someone who investigates a given reality but of someone who does theory.[9] He wants to modify language, that is thought and mind, in order to show what was in front of our eyes that we did not see. If a new theory is valid, this is why. The game of knowledge is played on the border between what is visible and what is invisible, between what is and is not sayable—the rest is consequence and outline. Correspondence-truth would be impossible to establish and therefore without sense if there were not something that would be true by simply being said.

Therefore, we should acknowledge that every "physics" needs a metaphysics (every psychology needs a metapsychology, etc.). As a matter of fact, every "physics" always contains a good or more often a bad metaphysics. I have learned this epistemological principle reflecting on Ernst Mach and his *Mechanics* which, emphasizing the metaphysics implied in classical physics, has had a liberating effect on the scientific mind, as Einstein's theory of relativity reveals.[10]

An authentic sense of being manifests itself in the correspondence between making sense and being true. In fact, it shows us that there is no being without thought, and that the principle of knowing is the self-presentation of being.[11]

But what is the problem? It is a matter of succeeding in thinking the real, of which we have a limited and contradictory experience (for example—it is actually more than an example—our mothers' miseries . . .), without losing our authentic sense of being, which consists of positivity and presence. When critique lacks the authentic sense of being, it becomes endless and does not lead anywhere.

Gustavo Bontadini, who taught me what metaphysics is, defines being as the "energy capable of rejecting nothingness from itself."[12] Can one say about this energy that besides the idea, we also have the experience? I think so, and in this I differ from what I have been taught. The experience of the relationship with the mother, which leaves in us not a memory but an indelible mark, is like a schema for our future experience. It provides the possibility of giving future experience a logical order. In this regard, that experience remains unique and unrepeatable. But this is not completely so, according to the tradition of speculative mysticism that speaks about a true experience of being.[13]

I differ from Bontadini's teaching on another point. According to him, an authentic sense of being is traceable also in Plato's doctrine of the *chora* (the original receptacle of everything from which the demiurge God will extract the universe) or in Aristotle's doctrine of the *hylé* (the shapeless and inert matter that precedes the creation of the universe thanks to God's pure act). For me the dualism of sky and earth in ancient cosmology, which puts the negative on the side of the earth, runs contrary to the right sense of being. This is because this dualism puts the negative on the side of generation, and consequently invalidates our relationship with the matrix of life and arouses an insurmountable suspicion regarding everything that concerns life. This specific suspicion destroys the value of sensory experience, disqualifying our feeling and enjoyment. These are the only experiences—and I am not the only one to assert this—which succeed in making immediate to us our sense of the positive and the present, of which it seems to me we could not have any idea otherwise.

In fact, we keep losing this idea. According to Emanuele Severino, a philosopher of Bontadini's school, the whole history of Western philosophy is "the vicissitudes of the alteration and, therefore, of the forgetting of the sense of being mentioned for the first time by the most ancient Greek thinking" (the author refers mainly to Parmenides's fragments). Severino also writes that the question of forgetting begins the moment that the opposition to the negative, which gives us the sense of being, ambiguously becomes a law that rules being as it were from the outside, ceasing to be an immanent power of being. (Severino refers to Aristotle's principle of noncontradiction, that is, a principle that is logical before being ontological.)[14]

In a way this thesis corresponds to my idea that our sense of being is connected to our experience of relationship with the matrix of life. The advent of the law of the father (patriarchy) superimposes itself on the positivity of the work of the mother. It separates logic from being, causing us to lose over and over again our sense of being.

The connection between the loss of the sense of being and the cultural repression [*rimozione*] of our relationship with the mother is not only a myth of origins. We can also read about this connection throughout the history of philosophy. I will give two examples.

One example is *the tendency to redouble* objects and values. The tendency to redouble the world of experience in an ideal world is well known because it has often been criticized by empiricists and positivists. But this is not exclusively the tendency of idealists. We can also find it in modern experimental science (and in those sciences that have taken it as their model). As a matter of fact, the laboratories and languages of modern physics seek a substitute for the ordinary world and ordinary language. In any case, it seems necessary that in order for us to know the reality of our experience, we must re-create it without obscurity and contradiction. Thus, it is necessary, for instance, to keep a distance from the society of common people and become a scientific society of specialists.

The philosopher Hans Kelsen, who developed his philosophy in the neopositivist Vienna Circle, explains the tendency to redouble as follows: "man evidently lacks full confidence in his own senses and his own reason."[15] Kelsen does not explain the reason for man's lack of confidence. I explain it in terms of the cultural repression [*rimozione*] of the old relationship with the mother. This distance from the matrix of life, in particular from our actual relationship with it, is too great. It takes away from us any trust in our passional and rational forces and in the possibility of putting them into a relation of useful collaboration. Consequently, we are in a condition similar to premature babies who are weak and entrusted to an incubator for their survival.

The second example of the tendency to redouble involves a passage from Descartes's "Third Meditation" in which he states that "it does not follow from the fact that I existed a little while ago that I must exist now."[16] Bontadini remarks that Descartes's passage shows the modern conception (that, to Bontadini, is a nihilist conception) of a being that "does not feel up to claiming for every being the right not to be overpowered by non-being."[17] I would say that what this passage shows is a nihilist conception of being that has lost the certainty of not being overpowered by nonbeing because it has silenced the female power that has given it life.

Strangely, Severino refers to the nihilist conception of being as a "being deprived of its virility":[18] perhaps this is because in patriarchal culture the power of the mother is represented only as phallic. Perhaps it is because virility is stolen from the mother, and consequently this theft must be hidden, together with the mother, obviously.

If we let the mother speak to us, from her, from our ancient relationship with her we could learn to fight nihilism, which is the loss of the sense of being.

Historically we see that philosophy has fought against two forms of nihilism. One form conceives being as originarily limited by nothingness and bound to end up in nothingness—a being that is absurdly indifferent to either being or nonbeing. The other form of nihilism separates being from thinking, both conceived reciprocally as independent from one another. (When I say that philosophy has fought against two forms of nihilism, I mean that philosophy has been a battlefield, or rather that philosophy has been torn between them.)

There is another form of nihilism I want to discuss. This nihilism conceives being as indifferent to being true or false. It is the nihilism of pretense-being, of copy-being. But it is a copy of nothing, it is a mise-en-scène, the reality of which is only a display that is *believed* to be true.

To begin it is necessary to bring to light this other form of nihilism against which an authentic sense of being also strives. The difficulty of beginning that I pointed out earlier comes from this form of nihilism. As I mentioned earlier, the decision to write about a specific subject does not bring order to my thoughts, but, instead, it causes an opposite reaction, and from beginning to end I am torn and uncertain. In fact, being, conceived as indifferent to being either true or false, cannot prescribe anything. The will to say what is true becomes useless, if not cumbersome. In relation to such a concept of being, the question of true or false is not relevant. The question of likelihood and credibility, instead, takes its place. It gives rise to a saying for which true being is not enough; actually it is not even of concern.

We obtain credibility by making what we say coincide with something already said or something sayable by others. So the mind thinks what has already been thought. That is, the mind does not truly think because thinking, which is an activity in a pure state, means by definition thinking the unthought. At the beginning of *The Passion according to G.H.*, Clarice Lispector, the great South American writer of Jewish Russian origin, talks about this coincidence as a kind of third leg, something for which one might feel a great need, but which would stop one from moving.

> Something's missing that once was essential to me and is so no longer. I don't need it anymore, as though I had lost a third leg that until then kept me from walking but made me a stable tripod. It's that third leg that's now missing. And I've gone back to being someone I never was. I've gone back to having something I never had before: just my two legs. I know that I can walk only when I have two legs. But I sense the irrelevant loss of the third one, and it horrifies me, it was that leg that made me able to find myself, and without even having to look.[19]

For a long time I have been struggling with this problem without understanding its true nature. Philosophy did not help because it seems to ignore this form of nihilism. Nevertheless, in the history of philosophy we can find some approximate examples of this form of nihilism, such as the renowned hypothesis of a malicious demon I have already mentioned. Descartes argues that we should assume the creature who deceived him skillfully was not God, who is the greatest good and the supreme source of truth, but a certain demon as malicious and powerful as he is cunning and fraudulent. This demon makes us think that the sky, the air, the earth, and everything we know to be true are false.

But as is well known, Descartes's fiction is a mere fiction. What I am talking about, instead, is a real fiction because it takes the place of reality. There is no way to discover a true sense of being, that is to say a reciprocal *interest* tying being to language. Figuratively speaking, this means that surely language can say either the true or the false, but it "prefers" to say the true (slips of the tongue, for instance, can prove this preference) and, vice versa, it means that being expresses itself in either way, but it "prefers" the truth.

I understood the significance of the nihilism of false being, of being presupposed to be indifferent to the true/false, when I thought over the conclusion of *The Passion according to G.H.* At the end of her itinerary, G.H. says:

> The world interdepended with me—that was the confidence I had reached: the world interdepended with me, and I am not understanding what I say, never! Never again shall I understand what I say. For how will I be able to speak without the word lying for me? How will I be able to speak except timidly, like this: life is itself for me. Life is itself for me, and I don't understand what I am saying. And, therefore, I adore . . .[20]

Why such exultation, I asked myself. I was doubly surprised because G.H.'s joy echoed in me deeply. Why? That joy comes from being certain that the real is not false, and it does not depend on us to be. Joy comes from being suddenly relieved of the fatigue of pretending; of pretending when we speak, when we listen, when we walk, when we love. Pretending life, in other words. Instead, it is not true that life requires pretending. It is when we realize this that all of a sudden that incomparable joy appears. We are grateful to finally rest on being, which needs neither words nor anything else we could add to it.

Lispector's position must not be confused with that of the dogmatic realism that defines reality as independence from thought. In

The Passion according to G.H. the independence of the real is obtained through language, which turns out to be the fruit of its failure:

> Language is my human endeavor. I have fatefully to go searching and fatefully I return with empty hands. But—I return with the unsayable. The unsayable can be given me only through the failure of my language.[21]

It is thus a question of arriving at a way of being that speaks for itself [*si dice da sé*], saying the unsayable that is in us in its pure presence. We can reach that being through the effort and the blockage of the word.

The Passion according to G.H. ends up reaching pure presence (the unsayable) through the failure of the regime of mediation (language). The result of *The Passion according to G.H.* is the same as that of the mystical tradition, masculine and feminine, although it is more feminine than masculine. In both cases, an extreme abbreviation that needs to be explicated succeeds in overcoming nihilism and in finding again a sense of being.

When a woman decides "to start telling the truth," a passage opens up between the presumed necessity to pretend and the absolutely unsayable. This passage seems to have been skipped over in G.H.'s journey and in the mystical itinerary. As a matter of fact, both of them aim at the unsayable, in order to make every mediation and every pretense fail together. This twofold and simultaneous failure corresponds to the point of view (supposing it can be called so) that gives being to the pure presence of being. Here every word sounds like a lie, according to the testimony of women and men engaged in this type of research.[22]

Now I would like to draw attention to something that is very common, but not banal. The feeling of a radical blockage of the word corresponds also to the viewpoint of many women, for whom putting into words and lying seem almost, and often are, the same thing. It is often this way, especially for those who mainly aspire to hearing and saying the true.

There is an absolute unsayable, and then there is a historically determined difficulty to say one's own experience. But the two unsayables, which in theory are distinguishable, if taken singularly may end up being inseparable. Or she does not want to separate them, as if foreseeing in the ordinary difficulty of speaking the prefiguration of the absolutely unsayable.

Historically speaking, this has been one path for the liberation of female thought. In order to fight against the hostility of patriarchal culture toward the self-signification of female experience, women have taken a road that is often difficult to follow, on which it is easy to break one's neck. The point is that even the other way, the gradual one, the way without shortcuts, is hard, although on it, failures may pass rather unnoticed. In fact, it is not a question of great human disasters, but, instead, of modest failures. Carolyn Heilbrun, an expert on women's (auto)biographies, evokes this type of blockage by pointing out how flat and reticent the narration of many women is when they tell about female existences, which are in themselves very exciting. "All of these autobiographies 'exploit a rhetoric of *uncertainty*.' . . . And in all of them the pain of the lives is, like the successes, muted, as though the women were certain of nothing but the necessity of denying both accomplishment and suffering."[23] I borrow from Heilbrun the invitation, cited above, "to start telling the truth."

A more circumscribed problem complicates the question of fiction taking the place of reality. What leads us to aim directly at the unsayable in order to come out of alleged reality, instead of aiming to start telling the truth? On the other hand, what too often makes those women who are instead engaged in the regime of mediation fail?

I offered an answer when I spoke of the difficulty of self-signification that women encounter in patriarchal culture. This is not a satisfactory answer because patriarchy, in its turn, finds support in women's difficulty in submitting to the necessity of mediation. As can be more easily observed in our society, speaking out on behalf of women is not formally prevented. What I mean is that patriarchy is also an effect and not only a cause.

So it is necessary to question this blockage. Here we must look for an answer within. The conception that being comes from nothingness and it is destined to nothingness is the typical nihilism of modern culture. It is also a false solution to the problem presented by the experience of becoming. Just as false is the solution of mimesis (the nihilism that gives to fiction the place of reality). The real problem is the lack of symbolic authority; that is, the authority to affirm what is. Language has this authority, and we make it ours by learning to speak.

Lacking this authority we do not necessarily lose linguistic competence, which is there, anyhow, simply to cover up the defect of another more basic competence that I call symbolic. Symbolic competence consists of having the sense of mediation and of its necessity. Human beings (said to be rational animals but more appropriately called symbolic animals) need mediation not only to know the far and the absent, but also the near and the present.

The expression "rhetoric of uncertainty" is quite appropriate. As a matter of fact, symbolic incompetence has repercussions at a linguistic level, causing in the female speaker an uncertainty about whether words can truly say what she wants them to say. This uncertainty makes her look for expedients to resolve the uncertainty, which, instead, make it more manifest, such as the emphasis put on more obvious things and the reticence with which more important things are advanced. The resolving expedient is ultimately a mimesis: a saying that ends up saying what others have said or would say, finding support in what they want to say.

This form of nihilism can also be traced back to the cultural repression [*rimozione*] of the experience of the relationship with the mother. She taught us to speak and she answered for language and its ability to say what it is. At the time we were learning to speak, the authority of language was inseparable from the authority of the mother. But the mother loses her authority in our adult lives, and this, I think, is the cause of the symbolic incompetence I discussed earlier. This lack of symbolic competence exists, perhaps, because there are some people, especially some women, me for instance, for whom there is no authority if it is not also authority of the mother. When the authority of the mother fails, so does a sense of reciprocal interest that passes between language and reality. Consequently, for them, words always turn out to be inadequate to say what is. Every mediation is disbelieved and disputed because of the weakness of this authority that needs to be continuously supported. Pretending, like criticizing, expresses this constant need to help and to dispute, endlessly unweaving and reweaving and unweaving again an endless web.

I ask myself: is it possible to stop the tiring, repetitive, and useless effort of this never-ending task we inherit from Penelope? Perhaps, if we become little girls again. Or perhaps it would be more realistic to translate into our adult lives the early relationship with the mother in order to experience it again as the principle of symbolic authority.

Chapter Notes

Chapter 2, page 18: The female relationship with the mother also includes the fact that a woman could become a mother, and many women do. I will not dwell on the event of becoming a mother, which is something that I myself have experienced and that in our culture is of great interest because it is believed to be absolutely the most important thing that could happen to a woman. I do not agree on this point. I believe that becoming a mother is symbolically relevant because it redefines the relationship of a woman with her mother in many ways: in terms of imitation and admiration or of envy, rivalry, revenge, or of loving obedience. The symbolic relevance of becoming a mother has as its background the originary relationship with one's own mother, and this is what I am talking about. I leave to each individual to make her own deductions on the meaning of her motherhood. Of those women who do not become mothers, one can logically think that they find no fault with maternal work. This would explain the feeling of strength and freedom emanating from some unmarried women in the past, such as "sisters" or "beguines."

Chapter 2, page 19: It is difficult *not* to see the opposition between realistic and symbolic, but it is necessary to do so in order to grasp the meaning of the maternal principle as I intend to explain it. In fact, it is difficult *not* to use this opposition to help define the meaning of "realistic" and "symbolic." However, as literature teaches us, there is a realistic symbolic. Novels are not based on axioms and rules of deduction, although the plots of some novels, like those by Ivy Compton-Burnett, are as connected in all their parts as a theorem is. How? They make principles and rules of deduction out of facts and desires. A realistic symbolic takes place when the real is signified more through its effects than through its representation, which normally happens in life just as in novels. Take a simple example: the recent Gulf War is changing people not in consequence of a true argument but as an effect of many arguments for which the possibility of making war is one of their presuppositions. The politics of women can also be considered a form of realistic symbolic because, without providing definitions and representations of being woman/man, it makes sexual difference operate in order to achieve women's freedom (contrary to its traditional result of nonfreedom). This is possible to do because, according to R. Jakobson's well-known theory, language obeys two principles: the metaphoric and the metonymic. See my *Maglia e uncinetto* [*Knitting and Crochet*] (Milan: Feltrinelli, 1981).

Chapter 2, page 22: On the desire to know as a sublimation of male love for the mother, the classic account is Freud, "Leonardo da Vinci and a Memory of His Childhood," *Works*, vol. 11, 63–137. Philosophers are just as likely as common people to think of knowledge as a growing approximation to an object that in itself remains unreachable or inexhaustible, and that resists the most elementary critique, as if it were not possible either to get close to or to move away from a goal considered unreachable. Freud's interpretation has the merit of restoring sense to a conception that is in itself illogical.

Chapter 2, page 25: With regard to the "sense of being," I value its positivity and presence (that are variously defined by others; for instance, as "appearance" or as "self-manifestation" by Edith Stein, and as "creativity" by Bergson). Heidegger would reject the idea of presence because it would make us understand being "with regard to a definite mode of time, the *present*" (Heidegger, *Being and Time* 22). This idea does not affect us if time is not a theater but, instead, it is the thinkability of becoming. That is, time is a mediator of our experience (just like language, in a way). Therefore, the present is, in relation to the past and the future, a punctual suspension of the necessity of mediation. To me, Heidegger also lacks the "sense of being" when he writes, "Da-sein is not something objectively present which then has as an addition the ability to do something, but is rather primarily being-possible" (ibid, 134). Let me be clear that "being-possible" is also something positive. However, by granting supremacy to "being-possible" instead of "being present," Heidegger turns the positivity of being present into a negative force, as revolutionary Western philosophy shows very often when the tendency toward realizations of the new turns into a force that destroys the positive notion of Da-sein (therefore, also of the notion of being-possible).

CHAPTER 3

The Word, a Gift from the Mother

Almost everybody, including me, thinks that the most important experience in our lives by far is the relationship with the mother in our first months and years of life.

Worded thus, this idea lacks precision and could be questioned. But I know of no objections that couldn't be overcome. As a matter of fact, the invaluable importance we give to childhood experience expresses a deep orientation of our culture that belongs to what Braudel calls the *longue durée*.[1] This history began to loom up at the beginning of modern times, and then asserted itself during Romantic culture. Even after the decline of Romanticism, it continued to develop up to, and most likely beyond, our own day.[2] In fact, it is a view that is practically unquestionable, though that does not mean immutable, for us. The endurance or change of this history does not depend on our arguments. We can enrich it; we can also try to give it its most logical form. That is, we can give it a form more revealing of the true than that which, mixed with other elements, is commonly, and rightly, believed to be expressed through this history. To this end, objections to the idea of the importance of childhood experience are necessary.

Although in general we are strongly convinced of the importance of our childhood experience, we do not know how to use it. We can investigate it, but we cannot use it. We are not able to make it truly ours in combination or interaction with other, later experiences, or to translate it into a knowledge that is as useful as the importance we give to it.

I am not the first person to state this fact. In the introduction to *Of Woman Born*, Adrienne Rich writes, "We carry the imprint of this experience for life, even into our dying. Yet there has been a strange lack of material to help us understand and use it."[3] The material to help us understand this experience is not lacking. Actually, it is growing. What we lack, instead, is the ability to use it.

I will illustrate by giving the general examples of disease and need. I exclude from need that which is caused by social injustice, because the only valid answer to injustice is to struggle against it. How can we respond, instead, to the need caused by disease, by handicap, by old age? Imitating little boys and girls [*i bambini e le bambine*] would be a good answer. Given even the least favorable conditions, boys and girls turn the state of need into a true laboratory to transform and know themselves and the world. However, for adults this is considered a humiliating response. We prefer other solutions, weaker responses. Why on earth is such a great and useful example of behavior, which we, furthermore, have registered in our personal histories, not culturally available?

What I have just stated is not exact. The aesthetics issuing from psychoanalysis teaches that art restores preverbal experience to us. I was thinking, instead, of a more ordinary availability and integration into the experiences of everyday life. As a matter of fact, art shares the regime of separateness that affects the condition of children. In the last hundred and fifty years, art and childhood have been increasingly isolated.

In addition to art, Winnicott considers religion and philosophy as offering keys for a possible restoration of early childhood experience. Consequently, he reconstitutes the triad of the life of the absolute spirit, described by Hegel.[4]

Like the great Melanie Klein, Donald W. Winnicott, psychoanalyst and pediatrician, is among those few who are able to speak of early childhood experience without isolating it from the rest of human experience. It is instructive even for those who are not interested in childhood to read his writing. Winnicott is a philosopher in the sense I mean: he can move from "physics," from correspondence-truth, to metaphysics, to the truth that is presented by the sense of words. He writes that "the world is being created anew by each human being, who starts on the task at least as early as the time of birth and of the first theoretical feed."⁵ Even the idea of a first theoretical feed is a beautiful philosophical invention.

There are at least two risks in the operation of integrating childhood experience into human experience. A well-known risk is that of reductionism, using as a master key what we have, or what we think we have, understood about childhood.

The other risk has been pointed out less often, but to me is more serious. This risk consists in considering our preverbal experience, that is, when the mother's body, mind, and desires were one with ours, to be the only true human experience, and all other experiences to be false and vain in comparison. This is an old mental phenomenon. Parmenides understood the sense of being as being one, motionless and positive. Consequently, as a fragment of his work states, he regarded the manifold and changeable world of experience as illusory and made up only of names.⁶

The people who run the second risk are those who reason about early childhood neither superficially nor sentimentally nor protected by their specialties. After all, these are the only people in a position to translate childhood experience. But it seems that once they learn the science of childhood, they consequently lose their interest in translating it.

What about Winnicott in relation to this? I do not know Winnicott well, but I will use his work to present a line of thought that otherwise would be too long. Winnicott undeniably belongs to the category of people just described, with the difference that he translates the "science" acquired in contact with the experience of early childhood. But Winnicott manages to translate this experience only partially.

Winnicott explains the idea that "the world is created anew by every human being" by saying that what the suckling re-creates depends largely on what the mother, who actively adapts to her child's needs, presents at the moment of creativity. If the child is not creative then, what the mother presents to her child has no meaning. This is a precise scientific theory in which we can also discern a cosmology and a theology. This theory varies its significance according to whether the child who constitutes a creating couple [*coppia creatrice*] with the mother is a girl or a boy.

But Winnicott goes on, and everything—theory, cosmology, and theology—suddenly falls apart when he writes, "We know that the world was there before the infant, but the infant does not know this, and at first the infant has the illusion that what is found is created."[7] Who is this "we"? Winnicott goes on to say that the child will arrive step by step at "an intellectual understanding of the fact of the world's existence prior to the individual's."[8] It cannot be denied that the existence of the world precedes that of the individual, and knowing this is a true achievement of the mind. Earlier Winnicott said that the creation of the world is not the work of the individual, but rather the work of the couple that he or she made with the mother. Winnicott seems to forget this now.

Winnicott adds that the child is now convinced, like "us," that the world exists independently of us, and that the experience of creating is an illusion of which the child preserves a trace. It is "the feeling . . . that the world is personally created."[9] That is better than nothing, I would add. Winnicott destroys what is best in his philosophy by positing the notion of the "we" who "know that the world was there before us." Who knows? Since when? From what is left of his philosophy, he develops a nihilist conception according to which "there is no direct contact between external reality and myself, only an illusion of contact."[10] To finish, Winnicott falls also into Parmenides's syndrome, from which the introduction of the "we" could not save him because it is the poor point of view of dogmatic realism and not the lucid and aware viewpoint that he supposes it to be. Although Winnicott has wonderfully reconstructed the point of view of childhood (we should not forget that), he pays for having arbitrarily introduced into it the judgment pronounced by the monstrous "we," generalizing it to the whole of human experience. It is an illusion.

The point to which we must return and attend is, of course, the creating experience of the origins. This does not refer to a subject in the ordinary sense but to the experience of a subject in relation with the matrix of life; it is a subject that can be distinguished from the matrix but *not from its relation to it*. Therefore, it is not exactly a relation between two, but a relation of being with being. This is how I suggest we think of it. But this relation is neither tautological nor self-reflective. It seems to me that it is a dynamic relation that is correctly conceived according to the relation of being a part. In certain conditions, part-being [*essere-parte*] can enter into a creative relation with being as being [*essere-essere*].

A point that is evident in Winnicott's text, as in a thousand other texts of our culture, blocks our path into this theme. This is the fact (I call it this for the sake of brevity) that the point of view of the originary creating couple constituted by the little girl or the little boy in relation with the mother (mythologically speaking: I have already explained that it is not exactly a couple) is a point of view that gets lost and is replaced by the point of view of a solipsistic subject, the individual ("I"), or the collective ("we"). The solipsistic subject passes judgment on the early relationship with the mother, ignoring the fact that it itself possesses an original experience of that relation. It unconsciously despises its potential truth, which consists in being in itself an experience of an authentic sense of being. If these words have a sense . . . I find their sense in the mirror of mystical experience. I think that our inability to avail ourselves of childhood for the purposes and problems of human existence as a whole can be traced back to the loss of this originary point of view.

How can this loss be explained? It is easy to answer this question, but it is not easy to do it in a few words because the answer is spread across many theories, figures, rituals, uses, and throughout the centuries it takes on a thousand nuances. The answer can be roughly summarized as follows. Since culture separates itself and ourselves from nature (the agent of such separation being the father), it is also necessary that we separate ourselves from the mother. It is necessary that we turn our back on the experience of our relationship with the mother in order to enter the symbolic and social order. In other words, symbolic independence is necessarily paid for with the loss of the point of view of the couple creating the world.

Corresponding to this "fact," therefore, a structural characteristic of the symbolic order is the necessity of considering our experience of the relationship with the matrix of life as unable to signify itself and therefore not constituting a point of view. We can inquire into this experience, and we can also explain it, but only from a point of view and by means that are not appropriate because they are acquired from a symbolic order in which the former relationship with the mother does not and cannot take place anymore.

This would clearly explain the importance given to that early and unrepeatable experience and the impossibility of integrating it with other experiences.

All of this is very plausible, but it is not true. It is not true for the simple reason that we learn to speak from the mother or from the one in her place. We learn to speak not in addition to something or as a supplement but as an essential part of the vital communication we have with her.

The loss of the viewpoint of the original creating couple corresponds to no necessity, nor to any facts. Nonetheless, the necessity of separating ourselves from the mother to enter the order of speakers is so strongly represented in our culture that it has become self-evident. I think of my friend D.B., who brought up her two daughters and sons without a husband-father, and nonetheless is convinced that they learned to speak from him. Given facts clearly showed her that a mother can offer her son and her daughter a place of thirdness in symbolic existence. But those facts were not enough. They were never enough because correspondence-truth cannot stand by itself; it needs metaphysical (or if you like logical) truth. My friend D.B. did not realize that, just as being cannot be separated from thinking, so the matrix of life is not separate from the origin of the word.

Facts must be regarded in this light. The life we live before we know how to speak must be seen as life spent learning to speak. The moment of birth should be seen as the decision of the fetus [*nascitura*] to get out into the open and to renounce its intrauterine ease in order to have what it could not have there—that is, air and breath indispensable to phonation. As a result, intrauterine life must be seen as life listening to voices, first of all the voice of the mother, who is perhaps inviting the baby to imitate her voice, and therefore to want to be born.

Of course, this is something I made up; yet what I said about very early childhood has something true in it. I know very little about it; I know nothing more than an ordinary adult. But no particular competence is necessary to know that the first thing a pregnant woman does, once she has accepted that she is pregnant, is to *think* of her child [*creatura*]. So from the first moment of her relationship with the baby she creates a place of "thirdness," as Pierce calls the mode of being of signs.[11]

I know only one theory of language that answers to my theorem that the matrix of life is for us also the matrix of the word. This is Julia Kristeva's theory, which she explains in the first part of *Revolution in Poetic Language*. It is a rather complicated theory, but it is worth knowing. The crux of her theory is the concept of semiotic *chora*.

Chora is a Greek word with many meanings, among which is that of "receptacle." Plato uses it as a metaphor for the mother's womb to designate the real without either order or unity that precedes the work of God. For Kristeva, the *chora* is the receptacle (we cannot speak in terms of either time or place yet) in which the first processes of the life of signs develop. Kristeva calls the life of signs "signifiance."[12]

We must know that to Kristeva the life of signs has two modalities that are mutually heterogeneous: the semiotic and the symbolic. We obtain the symbolic by identifying a subject and its objects. Logically and chronologically, the semiotic comes earlier, and from a genetic point of view it corresponds to the life of drives of earliest childhood described by Melanie Klein. The semiotic consists of elementary functions that bind and orient the body of the baby in relation to the mother. At this stage there is no subject/object, and we cannot speak of an order either. But there are processes that have rhythm, and they follow a sort of regulation due to the biological and social constraints mediated by the mother's body.

Most of Kristeva's theory deals with the relations between semiotic and symbolic in poetic production, which we can set aside except for those parts emphasizing the importance of the semiotic not only for the acquisition but also for the actual life of language. But always from within the symbolic: in fact, the semiotic is practically contained in the symbolic and mediated by it. And for this reason, it is not directly accessible to us.

Kristeva repeatedly confirms that between semiotic and symbolic there is discontinuity and heterogeneity. They are separated by a border, the so-called thetic break, which it is possible to transgress only in extraordinary conditions. Art and dreams do it. Otherwise we would go mad. The thetic is the threshold of the symbolic order.

I do not agree with Kristeva on this part of her theory. Kristeva too seems to think that symbolic independence, the common ability to speak, is purchased necessarily with the loss of the point of view of the early relationship with the mother. In contrast with Kristeva, I assert that the symbolic order must begin to establish itself (otherwise it will never establish itself) in the relationship with the mother, and that the "break" separating us from her does not correspond to a necessity for the symbolic order.

Among Kristeva's arguments, I share the idea of the symbolic occultation of the semiotic. In other words, it is true that the constitution of the subject and the advent of articulated language have the effect of occulting the previous stage in the process of formation of the subject. This is the stage in which we actively and repeatedly put ourselves in relation with the mother—that is, with the world and with being.

We must ask ourselves what the cause of the occultation of the semiotic is. In my own history, in my judgment, the occultation of the semiotic—with all its characteristic manifestations: of the break, of almost irreversible loss (except in exceptional practices such as art, psychoanalytic therapy, or pathological regression)—this occultation was due to a lack of theory; the same lack of theory that stopped D.B. from seeing the work that she herself, together with her daughters and sons, had done. By theory, I mean literally the words that show us what is. Once I changed my relationship with my fellow women and my sex, I found the words and I saw the continuity of my life. During this change, which for a long time was almost unconscious, I never stopped discussing with my mother, or the one in her place, the conditions of my symbolic independence. And, according to what I have learned from the scholars I continue to cite, this was continuous with what I had done in my earliest childhood. Winnicott, for example, repeatedly writes about how the newborn [*neonato*] "comes to terms" with the mother.[13]

Consequently, I ask myself if some characteristics that Kristeva attributes to the thetic stage, that is, to the moment of the subject's identification, are not, instead, the characteristics of a sex, the male sex, and the characteristics of the patriarchal culture.

In relation to the so-called Oedipal triangle, or to the structure of the family according to Freud, Adrienne Rich writes that "The third term in the so-called Oedipal triangle is, in fact, patriarchal power."[14] This third term is neither the father in the flesh nor the father in a purely symbolic sense. Instead, it is a certain type of society and of organization of power. I find this formula correct.

Lacan, to whom Kristeva often refers, would have accepted this formula. Unlike Freud, Lacan does not consider historical reality an independent factor. According to Lacan, we are machined [*macchinati*] by the symbolic and history is the theater of that machination [*macchinazione*]. Similarly, I say that Kristeva's "thetic break" is patriarchal domination, where and when men arrogate the power of the mother to themselves. It also allows them to destroy the genealogy of the mother and to recruit women, one by one, into male genealogy, as Luce Irigaray teaches.[15] The theory of the thetic break tells this story, and as such it is true. But what this theory actually shows us is once again a determinate social order and history reduced to a theater, let's say, which allows us to see something else. I have taken my own case, which is surely not exceptional, being neither artistic nor pathological, as an example of a useful shuttling back and forth between the social order and the semiotic *chora* and vice versa.

Therefore, what remains valid of Kristeva's theory is the part that underlines the instance of the semiotic, that is, of the originary experience of the relation with the mother. The theory of the thetic break must be seen, rather, as the expression of a historically determined symbolic order. Therefore, the thesis according to which truth becomes possible with the thetic stage must be revised. This thesis is only valid for correspondence-truth. Similarly, the object of poetic art, which Kristeva considers "neither true nor false," must be considered, instead, as always true. Otherwise, there would be no poetic art.[16]

It seems to me that at this point the obstacle barring our way has been eliminated. The early relationship with the mother gives us a true and lasting point of view on the real. It is true not according to correspondence-truth but according to metaphysical (or logical) truth, which does not separate being and thought, and nourishes itself on the mutual interest between being and language. We learn to speak from the mother, and this affirmation defines who the mother is and what language is.

Now I would like to illustrate a practice to verify my assertions. They need to be verified because of the kind of society in which we live. In our society a woman might think that the mother is silent about very important things, tyrannical, and at the same time a thrall of power. The practice I want to illustrate consists in negotiating [*contrattare*] a symbolic existence with the mother. This practice verifies my assertions because it also modifies the existing social order and symbolic disorder. As a matter of fact, this practice restores to the mother something of the place she had in our childhood experience, and consequently it helps us find her again. If it were not because of the kind of society we live in, what I am saying would be evident. It is true that there would always be that kind of society in which the demonstration of the true is always to some extent a modification of what exists and making that true sayable is a conquest.

The practice of negotiating symbolic existence [*contrattazione*] derives logically from a presupposition that at first glance does not seem logical. What does not seem logical is the fact that knowing how to speak is a revocable gift from the mother, that the blockage of the word is the revocation of that gift, and that in order to get it back we need to come to terms with the matrix of life.

We could object to this by saying that social injustice deprives some people of the word and overendows others with it. This is independent of any negotiating relationships with the figure of the mother. Social injustice in relation to the gift of the word is the central theme of the *Lettera a una professoressa* (1967), which in Italy, as is well known, became one of the inaugural texts of the 1968 movement.[17]

It is true that there is such injustice, but I think that we cannot rectify social disorder without making symbolic order. The early childhood dependence on the mother is the object of a contempt that grants symbolic independence sufficient to preserve, but not to modify, what exists, as the events of 1968 suggest. We know that whoever wants to modify what exists must be able to speak, and (I repeat) we learn to speak from the mother.

This is an elementary negotiation or "coming to terms," as Winnicott better expresses it.

In order to find, or refind, the word lost either because of intrasubjective blockage or because of social circumstances, it is necessary to start by renouncing one's own symbolic independence—here defined as having mastery over the meaning of words and the faculty of preserving or changing that meaning—and being satisfied with what we can say, trusting to presence for the rest. In his well-known "Two Aspects of Language and Two Types of Aphasic Disturbances," Jakobson writes about a disorder that prevents the speaker from naming things that are in some way present or that have just been mentioned or drawn.[18] Since the blockage of the word has already deprived us of mastery over words, what we are exactly dealing with is not a question of having given up the word. Instead, it is a matter of accepting its loss and interpreting it as a way of finding again the point of view of the origins, that is, when we were dependent on the mother.

This is not the same as saying that we regress to our childhood condition. The possibility, and in some cases the necessity, of such regression exists, for example, in a therapeutic context. On the other hand, it is also possible to reactivate the viewpoint of childhood without regressing. Let us say that childhood dependence has never ceased. As a matter of fact, it is prolonged into dependence on the material and social environment. Environment is also the name that Winnicott and others give to the mother in relation to her child. There is nothing regressive in giving the first place to need, as long as it expresses itself in words and is not simply acted on.

Nevertheless, what I am describing might seem a surrender more than a negotiation. In fact, it is like the *"surrender"* of the alcoholic that Bateson describes in his profound comment on the liberation practice of Alcoholics Anonymous. According to this practice, the man or the woman who believes he or she can surmount the addiction to alcohol by his or her own will is destined to fail. But it is precisely the failure that can lead them to health. In fact, the first liberating step consists in recognizing one's own impotence and in entrusting oneself to a superior personal power ("God as *you* understand him to be") that will restore one's health.

Gregory Bateson remarks that before "surrendering," the alcoholic fights against the habit of drinking on the basis of the Cartesian dualism that separates conscious will or "self" from the remainder of the personality. The brilliant idea of Alcoholics Anonymous was to break the structure of this dualism with the first "step." And "Philosophically viewed, this first step is *not* a surrender; it is simply a change in epistemology, a change in how to know about the personality-in-the-world. And, notably, the change is from an incorrect to a more correct epistemology."[19]

This remark can also be applied to the negotiation of the child with the mother in order to have freedom of thought and freedom of speech in the world. It is a change of epistemology, a matter of thinking that the origin of life cannot be separated from the origin of language; nor can the body be separated from the mind. We must think this from the point of view in which their bond is not the object of a demonstration but a way of being, a habit.[20]

My friend F.C. asked me why we should negotiate symbolic existence with she who gratuitously gave us life. I agree with her when she says (I am summarizing her words) that a woman must turn, preferably, to the mother to receive what she needs. Why should we have to negotiate a good like that of knowing how to speak that you yourself theorize to be deeply rooted in the development of our relationship with the mother, from the very first moment when she begins thinking of her child [*creatura*]? Isn't perhaps the gift of the word potentially contained already in that very moment? Why should we read the blockage of the word as a revocation of the gift from the mother instead of looking for its causes outside the relationship with her?

These questions aim at the apparently illogical presupposition I mentioned earlier. We can answer those questions by saying that knowing how to speak cannot be given to us in the same way that life, the female (or male) sex, health, beauty, and so on, are given to us. These are goods we receive irrevocably from our mother, even if later on we can lose them in various ways. Language can be given to us only by means of that negotiation with the mother because language is nothing other than the fruit of that negotiation. Basically, knowing how to speak means knowing how to bring the world into the world, and we can do that in relationship with the mother, not separately from her. It is true that the blockage of the word can have causes that are external to such a relationship. But, nevertheless, we must refer to this relationship because external causes, such as violence suffered, poor education, emigration, and so forth, do irreparable damage to our ability to speak.

In *Course in General Linguistics*, Saussure writes that language is the social product of our faculty of speech.[21] Without social exchange there would be no language and our "faculty of speech" would perhaps be empty.[22] I think that the faculty of speech, which I call knowing how to speak, is also the fruit of an exchange with the mother. In language, which is the product of that exchange, the exchange with the mother and social exchange flow together, but language distinguishes itself structurally because of the characteristic of disparity [*disparità*].

The *authority* of language, like that of its speakers, consists in the capacity to make a particular use, which seems in itself arbitrary, a normative linguistic feature. In my opinion, this authority originates from the disparate exchange I have mentioned.

The characteristic phenomenon of language, which is to make a particular use become a general norm, is not exclusive to language. We can find the same phenomenon in the legal field. Kelsen describes what makes a binding contract by distinguishing between what has brought two or more people to draw up a contract and the binding character of it. Kelsen writes that "the binding contract and the procedure by which it is created, i.e. the expression of the agreeing intentions of the parties, *are two different phenomena*" (my emphasis).[23] In my view, this is also applicable to language. As I see it, the horizontal exchange among speakers, that is, among speakers on a par with one another, is connected with the acknowledgment of the authority of the mother (or the one in her place). Only the acknowledgment of the authority of the mother allows us to be in a disparate relationship with the real. It is this more elementary exchange that decides the characteristic normative force that language, and also single speakers, have.

The language we speak and our knowing how to speak are fruits, beyond the exchange among speakers, of an agreement with the real. This agreement is negotiated with the mother by exchanging our acknowledgment of her authority for the "faculty of speech." This idea about language and about our ability to speak is the object of an intuition that I strongly feel and that I continue to enrich with demonstrations. It is not a complete theory yet. In particular, I could not say anything definite about the way in which the social exchange connects with the mother. For the time being, I am more interested in listening to this intuition than discussing it.

Like any intuition, it has a firmer nucleus, but that is also the most elusive part to put into words. The nucleus contains three terms: the real-authority-sayability, along with their oppositions and all their other possible combinations. There are combinations that are infernal circles. There are vital combinations. The intuition I have had is felicitous because it has grasped a vital combination in which it becomes possible to say the real as it frees itself from self-repetition and from becoming always other than itself. This combination is governed by a principle forming the heart of my intuition. The principle says that logical order is neither given a priori nor it is conventionally invented. It takes shape as an obedience to necessity.

Chapter Notes

Chapter 3, page 38: My brief remarks on the relations between "part" and "whole" are too few and fragmented. In language these relations are varied and characteristic. Perhaps it is only by analyzing these relations that we could see how the symbolic differs from the physical and the logical. On this subject I recommend R. Jakobson, "Parts and Wholes in Language," *Selected Writings II* (Paris: Mouton, 1971), 280–84. Among the relations part/whole, I include the participative opposition of structural linguistics, between A, on one side, and A + not A, on the other. See K. Togeby, "Theodor Kalepky et les oppositions participatives," *Immanence et structure* (Copenhagen: Akademisk Forlag, 1968), 45–50. Perhaps this relation contains the principle of symbolic independence. It expresses the autonomy and at the same time the partiality of the part. In the past, when I wrote *Maglia o uncinetto* [*Knitting or Crochet*] (1981), I thought that the emblematic relation of the symbolic was that of the part for the whole. It appears to me that Jakobson drew the same conclusion in the aforementioned text.

Chapter 3, page 42: Freud's and Lacan's different positions on history stand out in their respective theories of femininity. At the end of his lecture on femininity, Freud cautions that "[it is not] always easy to distinguish what should be ascribed to the influence of the sexual function and what to social breeding." (*Standard Edition of the Complete Psychological Works*, vol. 22, 132). On the other hand, Lacan tends to emphasize the coincidence between historical condition and theoretical reason. "The sexed being of these not-whole women does not involve the body but what results from a logical exigency of speech. Indeed, logic, the coherence inscribed in the fact that language exists [. . .] requires this one by one." J. Lacan, *Seminar XX: Encore*, 1972–73, trans. Bruce Fink (New York: W. W. Norton, 1998) 10. "It is as a result of the same mechanism [the identification of the child with the mother's want-to-be] that women in the real order serve . . . as objects for the exchanges required by the elementary structures of kinship." (Lacan, *Écrits: A Selection*, trans. Alan Sheridan [New York: W. W. Norton, 1977], 207.) My theory is closer to Lacan's than Freud's. I do not think that history could be seen as an independent factor because of the cultural codes governing it and us. However, my theory differs from Lacan's because I think that we can create a symbolic by introducing unexpected factors into the social-symbolic order.

Chapter 3, page 43: My thesis is very simple. I assert that we learn to speak from the mother. I like the fact that this is common knowledge, at least in its enunciation. To be more precise, my thesis is that being (or having) body and being (or having) language take shape together [*insieme*] and that the work of the mother consists precisely in creating that whole [*insieme*] of body and language. Medieval chronicles tell us that the emperor Frederick II performed an experiment on language to prove his thesis that people would begin to speak spontaneously either Hebrew, Greek, or Latin. Frederick put some newborns [*neonati*] under the care of wet nurses who were not allowed to speak to the babies. The experiment failed because all the newborns died. Among the various theories denying that one learns to speak from the mother I was struck by Elisabetta Rasy's *La lingua della nutrice* [*The Language of the Wet-Nurse*] "Babies, after a period of muteness, lose their idiom; that is, they lose the rich and particular language they share with their wet-nurse which, according to Jakobson, has a psychotic character. It is when babies lose their idiom that they are born into the symbolic order and language; and the woman, who can always be a wet-nurse, maintains the idiom" (Roma: Edizioni delle donne, 1978), 22. Elisabetta Rasy seems to echo

Jacques Lacan. I am specifically referring to what he writes in "On a question preliminary to any possible treatment of psychosis": "It is . . . in the failure of the paternal metaphor, that I designate the defect that gives psychosis its essential condition" (J. Lacan, *Écrits*, 215).

Chapter 3, page 43: I have spoken of a practice of elementary negotiating symbolic existence with the mother without saying what this practice consists of. What I have in mind is the practice of disparity [*disparità*] in the women's movement: "it is necessary to make the maternal figure significant to the female as a figure of origin so that female difference can signify itself for itself, in full view of society, and be for every woman a principle of knowledge, and transforming power, with respect to the given reality. The originary significance of sexual difference [. . .] is activated by practicing disparity among women and entrusting oneself by preference to a fellow woman in facing the world." The Milan Women's Bookstore Collective, *Sexual Difference*, trans. Patricia Cicogna and Teresa de Lauretis (Bloomington: Indiana University Press, 1990), 116. While this practice modifies the patriarchal codes of relationships among women, at the same time it modifies women's relationship with the figure of the mother. The idea that the demonstration of the true is always in some way a modification of the real appears for the first time in the history of Western philosophy with Giambattista Vico and his principle "verum ipsum factum."

Chapter 3, pages 43–44: As I conceive it, the knowing how to speak that effectively accompanies the modification of what exists is essentially free of contempt for the childhood condition and free of aversion to the mother. Therefore, it conforms to the symbolic order of the mother. It is not a question of knowing how to speak according to the art of rhetoric, although there is a way to make of this art a sort of initiation into knowing how to love the mother and knowing how to remain within her order. Now that I have finished my book, looking back on it, I am sorry not to have developed my research in the direction of knowing how to speak. For instance, I wrote that a social disorder cannot be corrected without making symbolic order; is it perhaps because any social disorder (class division, sexist discrimination, excess of power of the market) ends up creating symbolic disorder? Or is it perhaps because the very attempt to correct injustice risks symbolic disorder? An extreme example of this could be the Cambodian revolution of Pol Pot. All of this requires further reflection. Instead of going in that direction, I have started from the blockage of the word, because this stood in my way. Perhaps I had no choice.

Chapter 3, pages 44–45: In my text there is a contradiction. First I say that the blockage of the word must be interpreted as a return to dependence on the mother. Then I say that I am not proposing a regression because the state of need in our life is permanent, and to put need in first place is not regressive as long as the need is expressed in words. Now, was not the loss of the word, perhaps, the cause of the problem? The contradiction disappears if we take into consideration that in the dependence on a given context there is a metonymic way of speaking, without symbolic independence from the world. This is an impoverished way of speaking, as R. Jakobson writes in "Two Aspects of Language and Two types of Aphasic Disturbances," but it is adequate to the expression of need.

Chapter 3, page 46: *Mettere al mondo il mondo* [Bringing the World into the World] (Milan, Italy: La Tartaruga, 1990) is the title of a book of philosophical investigations to which I contributed and whose authors are known under the name of Diotima. I gave this title in contradiction, one might think, with my undertaking not to make a metaphor of the work of the mother, if we do not include in her work her teaching us to speak. In fact, "bringing the world into the world" is in no way metaphorical. It is exactly what we do together with the mother, or the one in her place, when we learn to speak.

Chapter 3, pages 46–47: In many ways the so-called mother tongue is an obstacle to signifying the female subject and her experience. The lexicon lacks terms to name what women are and do. Grammatical rules do not consider the presence of feminine subjects, as can be seen, for instance, in the family group where the agreement of the plural must be in the masculine form. See Luce Irigaray, *Thinking the Difference* (New York: Routledge, 1994), 27, 41–58. Since language is a social product, it reproduces in this way a historical condition of the female subject in the system of social relations. However, we cannot reduce language to a product since language in its turn produces society and this originates from the exchange of life and word with the mother. As such, language is able to effectively help women in their coming to consciousness and in beginning to speak (for themselves). Facts show this too. Therefore, I am against any modification of language *ope legis* [by the law]. It is not necessary, and it would be an unfortunate solution. "Eppure la lingua ci è madre" ["And Yet Language Is Mother to Us"] is the wonderful title of a short essay on this topic written by three schoolteachers and language scholars. Vita Cosentino, Francesca Graziani, and Gabriella Lazzerini, "Eppure la lingua ci è madre," *Cooperazione educativa* (Florence: La Nuova Italia, May 1990): 14–18.

CHAPTER 4

Or the One in Her Place

Many times when I talked about the mother I added: or the one in her place. While I was writing, I said to myself that I would write a later chapter about what takes the place of the mother in our lives. I tried to name some of these possible substitutes such as the father, God, love, money . . . But I realized that these figures tell a story that does not correspond to my own, except for the fact that I have adapted myself to male culture. Those figures do not restore to me the viewpoint of the origins, but, instead, they give me the male viewpoint on the origins. By that I do not mean that women per se are without God or love, just to mention two substitutions marking women's existence. I mean only that we know very little about the way in which God or love would restore the viewpoint of the origins to a woman, supposing that they actually could give it back to her, instead of giving her a male point of view; whereas we know much, very much, of the way in which those figures restore the viewpoint of the origins to men.

Therefore, I must explain the one in her place as an operation before considering the results. Obviously, the formula in question refers to the well-known and wonderful fact according to which the biological mother can be replaced by other figures without causing the loss of the fundamental characteristics of the mother's relationship with her child [*creatura*]. In this fact, we can see the irrelevance of the natural element and the exclusive relevance of a structure that can be filled with any type of content. On the contrary, in this fact I read the symbolic predisposition of the mother who allows others to substitute for her without damaging or seriously damaging the work of creation of the world that she accomplishes with her child [*creatura*].

We can explain this symbolic predisposition of the natural mother by considering that a woman can become a mother or not, and, in any case, always remains the daughter of her mother, so that every natural mother is already a substitute.

So there is a structure. It is the structure of the maternal continuum that from within, through my mother, her mother, her mother, and so on, refers me back to the beginning of life. This structure, though, is too often misrecognized in its effects and its original characteristics of bridging nature and culture.

The first interpretation of sexual difference is among the effects of this structure. In fact, the female child [*creatura*] is situated at a central and at the same time conclusive place on the continuum (unless she reopens it if she in turn becomes a mother), whereas the male child is outside this continuum. He is symbolically excluded the very moment the mother comes to know his sex. Therefore, sexual difference is present from the origins of the relationship with the mother. For that reason sexual difference cannot be reduced either to sexual dimorphism, on the one hand, or to a cultural effect, on the other, such as the opposition sex/gender that gives rise to an erroneous understanding. The opposition sex/gender has been taken up by some parts of feminist thought, but this opposition is part of the male project in remaking and supplanting the work of the mother.[1]

We must notice that what is valid for the mother in terms of her availability for substitution is not valid for the child (whom I call *la creatura* according to the common use of the word, but keeping in mind that the child is part of a creating relationship [*relazione creatrice*], and this is characterized by sexual difference).

Unlike the mother, the child [*creatura*] is not in the place of the other, and it does not allow itself to be substituted. In compensation, it is able to accept substitutes for the mother. This is one of its most ordinary qualities, yet it is as wonderful and alarming as the story of the scientist who plunged himself up to the neck in a pond and managed to be taken, or to have his head taken, for the mother duck by a brood of ducklings.

I believe that this ability to accept substitutes for the mother corresponds to the operation that early philosophers call "saving the phenomena." That means interpreting our experience as real instead of looking at it as an appearance hiding something else or as a deceptive pretense.[2]

I have already mentioned Parmenides. From the fragments of his work one comes to the conclusion that he denied all reality to phenomena except the reality of their illusory appearance, because they present themselves as being and nonbeing at the same time, whereas being must present itself as pure positivity. Philosophers after him, beginning with Plato and Aristotle, posed the problem of how to "save the phenomena." They wondered how the instance of positivity of being could be safeguarded without having to draw the conclusion that the world of experience is unreal. They managed to do that by splitting the real into a world of becoming and an immutable world. The world of becoming is the world of our experience, and it is a prey to the contradiction of being and nonbeing. But it is not absurd and unreal. It is not equivalent to nothing because of its relationship with the immutable world. Philosophers understand the relationship of the world of becoming with the immutable world in various ways: as a relationship of participation, of causality, of emanation, of creation . . .

As I have already mentioned, I reject only what in this philosophical systematization is dictated by the male will to appropriate the power of the mother and to replace her work. Taking this distinction into consideration, it follows that "saving the phenomena"—that is, assuring the reality of the world of our experience in spite of what in it appears to be senseless and unsatisfactory—is equivalent to connecting the present experience to the originary relationship with the mother and reading that experience through that relationship, just as the ducklings in the pond recognize the absurd head of the scientist, Lorenz, as real because of the authentic logical operation of putting his head in the place of the mother.

Let's go back to our ability to accept substitutes for the mother, and examine how fundamental this ability is for the operation of saving the phenomena. Part of this ability is a tendency of our mind that is more often noted in its pathological manifestations than in this positive function. I am referring to *fixation*, which keeps intact in our mind something of the primordial relationship with the matrix of life, something that functions as an anchor in the series of substitutions.

When I followed Freud's text on the theme of fixation I discovered that, strictly speaking, he does not think of it as a pathological condition per se. In the "Case of Schreber" Freud writes of the process of repression, divided by him into three phases, that "the first phase consists in *fixation*, which is the precursor and necessary condition of every 'repression.' Fixation can be described in this way. One instinct or instinctual component fails to accompany the rest along the anticipated normal path of development, and, in consequence of this inhibition in its development, it is left behind at a more infantile stage." Freud goes on to write that what happens is that the libidinal current that has fixed itself in such a way acts on the evolving psychic context as if it were a repressed content, that is, a content that has become unconscious. But we have seen that instinctual fixation is not such because it is an originary phenomenon (even if it is not "normally" expected). Freud also writes that what determines the outcome of the third phase of the process of repression lies in the instinctual fixations. "The third phase, and the most important as regards pathological phenomena, is that of failure of repression, of *irruption*, of *return of the repressed*. This irruption takes its start from the point of fixation, and it implies a regression of the libidinal development to that point."[3]

Fixation, then, is not a determinant for the manifestations of a mental illness, which have other causes, but for the type of illness: for the "choice" of neurosis. From this we can infer that there are many types of fixation corresponding in some way to different pathologies traditionally known as hysteria, obsessive neurosis, and paranoia. On the other hand, once fixation is freed from pathological connotations, it can be assimilated to a characteristic of the primary relationship with the mother. Instead of evolving, this characteristic stays the same, and, in psychic life, it comes to constitute a factor of resistance to the substitutions for the mother—not every aspect of the mother can be substituted.

I maintain that it is thanks to fixation that substitutions are possible, and they provide a place for the symbolic. As a matter of fact, it is due to fixation that the possible substitutes for the mother are recognizable as such, which can consequently restore her to us in the present. They represent her to us in the full significance of re-presenting [*ri-presentare*].

Perhaps without fixation our life would be an endless deportation to an empty desert, or vice versa, to a desert full of senseless things in which we would wander, unhappy about what we have lost without even feeling that we have lost something because we have forgotten our original experience and are totally incapable of recalling it in our present.

In other words, what in us remains fixed to the mother functions as something immediate that needs the mediation (of substitutes) for us to remain mindful [*esserci presente*] of such immediacy. At the same time it allows us to recognize good substitutes, according to a circular structure typical of every mediation and, first of all, of language.

I will use another image to explain that the fixation on the mother acts within us like a grain of sand in a pearl oyster, activating the circular structure characteristic of mediation, and consequently giving rise to the symbolic dimension.

In my opinion, it is crucial to understand that substitution is equivalent to restoration. Certainly this understanding was important to me. As a matter of fact, I had lost the sense of correspondence of word to being because, as I reconstructed it later, every possible substitution of the mother functioned in my life as the opposite of her restoration.

If I had to say how this happened, I would answer that it had to do with school. Luce Irigaray writes of schooling as a deportation for the little girl, or rather as a kidnapping and rape. She compares schooling with the rape of Kore, Demeter's daughter, by the God of the Underworld.[4] In school, little by little I lost the capacity for original thought. When I say original thought, I do not have in mind an individual thought, although thinking always requires, of course, an engagement in the first person, which is something that school usually asks for and that it got from me. What I have in mind, instead, is the thought that has its resource and its end in what I know. I have in mind the type of thought for which the experience that needs to be explained and its explanation are in a circular relation, which shows by means of this circularity how experience and explanation have the same principle—thus making us understand that being and thought are co-originary.

But I already knew that mediation is the restoration of the immediate. I learned that at the school of philosophy. Why, then, did I find it so difficult to apply this principle to myself and to my thinking?

The answer is not easy. A first approximate answer that might be valid is what I said earlier about the "difficulty of beginning." To sum it up, in my search for original thought I fell into a kind of philosophical trap. I used to "save the phenomena" by going back to a male point of view on the origins instead of going back to the creative viewpoint of the origins in which being and thinking coincide. So I did not actually save the phenomena, and this made me feel as if everything was fake. Mediations were necessary to save the mise-en-scène and not my experience, which at times did not seem worth saving and at others seemed too exalted to put into words. But in other moments, it was not necessary to pretend any more. Every effort and necessity of mediation disappeared. Reality had become a sensible and enjoyable presence. The reality of the world of experience was not better assured, though, by this procedure than by that of adopting the viewpoint of others. As a matter of fact, these procedures are two sides of the same coin. The two procedures blended together, creating an imaginary world in a sort of female or hysterical version of "redoubling" of the world typical of philosophical and scientific tradition.

Of course, I am talking about hysteria that is female by definition. Although there are a number of women who are not hysterical at all, I want to show that the relationship between hysteria and being a woman is in the etymology of the word, and it corresponds to a correct intuition.

Male culture has always paid much, although not always benevolent, attention to hysteria. I have nothing to add to the descriptions of hysteria that have been given so far. What I want to say about hysteria concerns its meaning: what the word means.

As in other neuroses, we must go back to fixation in order to define hysteria. In hysteria as in other cases, fixation per se is not pathological. What is hysteria before becoming pain and disorder? It is a complete attachment to the mother such that it cannot accept having her substituted. Previously I mentioned that fixation shows that not every aspect of the mother can be substituted. In the case of the hysterical woman, nothing of the mother can be.

If we observe hysterical behavior, this characteristic of hysterical fixation is apparent. In fact, the hysterical woman does not seem herself to be attached to anything. She is always grafted onto the desire of others, but in a way that sooner or later makes clear that she has in mind the desire of the other not for the other but as nourishment for her own feeling, whether suffering or enjoyment.

But the deep aversion toward the mother was an obstacle to overcome in order to grasp the true characteristic of hysterical fixation. In his 1959–60 seminar Lacan said, "The behavior of the hysteric, for example, has as its aim to recreate a state centered on the object, insofar as this object, *das Ding*, is, as Freud wrote somewhere, the support of an aversion. It is because the primary object is an object which failed to give satisfaction that the specific *Erlebnis* of the hysteric is organized." And the "primary object" and the German *das Ding*, the thing, correspond to the mother.[5]

In fact, the hysterical woman turns body and soul against the mother. For instance, think of the hysterical arch. This is the opposite of the curled-up position of the fetus [*feto*] in the womb, it is literally turned over. Think of the deaf revolt of many women against any female authority. Think of the recriminations for the little love they say they have received instead of seeing how having been given life is already an ocean of love, and the only problem is, instead, their own capacity to contain that love.

This widespread aversion toward the mother stopped me from understanding the nature of hysterical fixation that is predicted in psychoanalytic theory until I understood the very reason for that hostility. The hysterical woman detests her mother because the latter is a substitute for the mother. I have already explained how the natural mother can also be considered a substitute. The typical female attachment to the mother corresponds to a love that is not for her own mother, but for a sequence of mothers. That is, it is a love for that structure that makes of every little girl the inner fruit of an inside of an inside [*il frutto interno di un interno di un interno*], and so on to the limits of the universe. I remember the fantastic cosmology of a little girl student of mine. She thought that we are at the center-base of a world from which, looking up, we see the inside of the round heavenly border. To her that world was the Earth, which she had learned was "round." When I tried to give her the most current interpretation of the phenomena, she held her own by saying "my mother thinks that too."

It is in this sense that the term *hysteria*, from the Greek word for *womb*, corresponds to a correct intuition and this should be preserved, despite the reductive or negative connotations. Hysteria interprets the female relationship with the matrix of life—no matter at this moment what the quality and cost of such interpretations. Hysteria interprets sexual difference.

So I have partly answered the earlier question about why the symbolic order, which develops through substitutions-restorations of the primordial experience of the relationship with the mother, operates, as I see it, as a falsification of that experience and as a loss of originality. My difficulty in practically mastering the structure of an original thought, of which as I have already said I knew the theory, reflects the characteristic of hysterical fixation, which consists of an attachment to the mother that does not tolerate substitutes, such as the well-known spool with which little Hans used to play when his mother was not around.

But my explanation is not complete. The fact that the hysterical woman responds with aversion toward the mother as an attempt to find symbolic independence, a very widespread and misleading choice, is due to the symbolic disorder characterizing patriarchal societies. The symbolic disorder of patriarchal societies does not need to be demonstrated because the structural characteristics of these societies express it. Patriarchal societies originate from the exchange of commodities, signs, and women, who are assimilated to commodities and signs. It is not explained whether and how they learn to speak.[6]

In our culture, the typical female attachment to the mother, which is internal and without possible substitutes, does not have a symbolic translation. This puts many women in a difficult body-against-body relation with the mother.

One might object that not all women are hysterical or have a tendency to hysteria. In fact, what characterizes hysterical women in comparison with other women? It seems to me that unlike the other type of woman, the hysterical woman makes an expressive "choice." That is, she "chooses" to express her attachment to the mother even when the appropriate symbolic means to signify it are missing. Therefore, she expresses her maternal attachment with her body, at the risk of falling into the hands of functionaries of the symbolic order such as fathers, priests, doctors, judges, legislators, intellectuals.

The difficulty lies in distinguishing the expressive choice of the hysterical woman from its consequences of subordination to male power so that this choice can be affirmed without those consequences. How do we perform this difficult operation? In the past, I thought and wrote that the problem could be solved by giving to female fantasies a real world, this real world of ours. I talked about a possible coincidence of the two worlds in the same way that the many sides of a cube coincide with one another. Now I see that this is not the solution, but it is already an effect, perhaps the most important effect, of the achieved solution.[7] Following the same line of thought and trying to reach an effective solution, I can now say that the symbolic order begins for the hysterical woman the moment she recognizes in the woman who brought her into the world the one who introduces her into the maternal continuum. As Melanie Klein taught us, the symbolic order begins with recognition.[8]

So the symbolic order begins for the hysterical woman, as for everybody else, by accepting the substitution of the mother, or it would be better to say, by recognizing that the substitution is a restoration. But with the stipulation that in this type of attachment to the mother, the substitution-restoration activating the typical structure of an original thought is never a substitution of the mother with something other than her. The mother in the flesh will be in her place in the way, let's say, a word is in place of its meaning. What is my problem, then? The problem is that I argue in terms of substitutions that are currently used to explain how we resolve the original bond with the mother, whereas concerning the "hysterical" attachment perhaps I should take into consideration the category of part-being that characterizes the originary relationship, but that does not make us think of independence at all.

The problem can be solved if we manage to think of a "substitution without substitutes" for the mother in agreement with the structure of the maternal continuum. This is possible because a "substitution without substitutes" exists: it is the language we speak, the first language we learned. In fact, the words of this language do not substitute for other words. Certainly they "substitute" for things, but without putting anything in their place.

Maybe for the hysterical woman the mother tongue is the only thing that can stay in the place of the mother, just as speaking is the activity that seems to account better than any other for the typical female relationship with the mother.

This thesis also finds a sort of evidence in female behavior. I am thinking of the *talking cure* invented by Anna O., about whom Breuer together with Freud wrote. This cure is at the origin of psychoanalytic practice.[9] I am thinking of the practice of consciousness-raising [*autocoscienza*] in the political movement of women, which reproduced some aspects of the female relationship with the mother.[10]

In support of that thesis, or perhaps it would be better to say in illustration of it, I will tell how I attained again the capacity for original thought. I will not tell the whole process but just how I reached the shore. I found it in this thought addressed to myself, when I realized that I had in mind what was all around me, and I could say it all as long as I passed by way of something that others also had in mind.

Once I formulated that thought, I felt an extraordinary relief comparable to the exultation that the positive resolution of a long period of uncertainty gives, as we read in sea novels (and perhaps that's why I spoke of reaching the shore).

In order to plumb the meaning of this discovery, I formulated it in different ways, and I verified their equivalence by logical means together with the verification of inner affect, which proved to be lasting and provided a kind of assistance to the work of the mind. Many things I have written in this chapter and some of those written in the previous one are the fruits of this exercise of reproducing the idea that I truly have in mind what is essential, and none of that is unsayable as long as I say it passing by way of what others also have in mind.

Even the form of my writing, almost from the very beginning of this book, obeys this principle. I use the term *principle* because it fulfills the function of a principle, namely the direct expression of my knowing how to love the mother. It is the fruit and the goal of that elementary negotiation that I described in the previous chapters and that has unconsciously occupied a good part of my life. Ordinary and secondary negotiation with women and men similar to me now takes the place of negotiation with the mother.

Regarding the obligation to pass by way of what others have in mind, some people might think that in this writing I find a way out quickly. It is true that I am not dwelling much on the well-established rules of demonstrative reasoning. For that reason, this writing will not seem to be much different from my previous writings where I used to oscillate almost without any criteria from my subjection to the rules of others to an overbearing effort to say things in my own way. To me, the present writing differs from my previous writing as day differs from night. I admit that, seen from the outside, it might seem just a shade of difference, just as dawn might appear to be a shade of light if seen from the outside. It must be said that the principle in question can be translated, in practice, in many ways between two extremes. At one end, we pass by way of rules already in force and generally followed. At the other end, we give ourselves up to the necessity of mediation without having determined its modes yet. Between these two extremes the criterion is to accord respect to the rules along with fidelity to what a woman has in mind. Clearly this accord does not consist in a compromise but in activating a relation of mutual empowerment so that the sayable I have in mind will increase with the observance of the rules.

Therefore, there are no absolute norms but only rules that are more or less appropriate in obtaining this result. After all, my closest social context is constituted by a female society in which it is as important as it is difficult to determine the modes of mediation. As a matter of fact, to us women, nothing of what belongs to a female experience can be excluded from sayability. This explains the unruly appearance of this writing: in fact, it obeys rules that are not known or established yet (if this makes sense—which it does to me).

I have been speaking of female society, whereas the principle of mediation refers to women and men and requires me to keep in mind [*tener presente*] what women and men have in mind [*hanno presente*]. This formulation is correct as long as the order of the word is observed, too: women come first because the principle took shape from the necessity of keeping in mind and respecting what women like me have in mind and respect (beginning with those to whom I am attached). Apart from other considerations, it is logical that women come first since I knew too well the rules set by men, and those rules did not ask me to formulate any principle. As a matter of fact, in order to find and respect those rules, I did not need either a symbolic order or original thought.

The rather frequent fact that women, the mother to start with, often conform to men's will is not an obstacle to my principle. Mine is a formal principle and not one of content. The symbolic effectiveness of this principle consists in the act of keeping in mind what counts for another woman, first of all the mother. I understood this point when I read *Persuasion* by Jane Austen, a conflictual love story similar to its contemporary *I Promessi Sposi* (*The Betrothed*) by Manzoni. Don Rodrigo's arrogance corresponds in *Persuasion* to the class differences that are authoritatively explained to Anne Elliot by Lady Russell, who is in the place of the mother for her. At the end of the story love triumphs, and the two lovers comment on their experiences. Anne Elliot says to Captain Wentworth,

> I have been thinking over the past, and trying impartially to judge of the right and wrong, I mean with regard to myself; and I must believe that I was right, much as I

suffered from it, that I was perfectly right in being guided by the friend whom you will love better than you do now. To me, she was in the place of a parent. Do not mistake me, however. I am not saying that she did not err in her advice. It was, perhaps, one of those cases in which advice is good or bad only as the event decides; and for myself, I certainly never should in any circumstance of tolerable similarity, give such advice. But I mean, that I was right in submitting to her, and that if I had done otherwise, I should have suffered more in continuing the engagement than I did even in giving it up, because I should have suffered in my conscience.[11]

Scholars of Jane Austen ask themselves: what is the secret of her perfect novels that have been loved and admired by readers and literary critics for almost two centuries? What is the secret of the great novels she wrote without having a literary model and in spite of her modest formal education and her ordinary provincial life? I think that Jane Austen's secret has to be sought in the symbolic order of the mother with which she intimately complied. This has given her language and culture, and it has made her speak with extraordinary conviction.

Therefore, the principle of necessary mediation is, for me and to my mind for every woman, a principle of mediation that is female in the first place. In fact, as Jane Austen shows, what is involved here is the overcoming of every aversion toward the figure of the mother. Above all, overcoming that aversion does not mean that we put man in place of the mother in order to love or hate him instead of her. On the contrary, it means recognizing her and accepting her authority.

As I have already said, it is not a principle of content, but instead it is a formal one. In fact, passing by way of what others have in mind in order to say what I have in mind corresponds in the most elementary way to speaking. Linguistic exchange among speakers can be regarded as a way of getting out of the perfect identity of oneself with oneself in order to come into existence in the *common place*. The common place reforms itself because everyone is available to represent things as a function of the other, or as a function of what the other has in mind. But how does one know what the other has in mind if not from their words? Isn't this a vicious circle? Yes, we fall into a circle, but this is not vicious because the structure of mediation is circular.

Still, if it is true that we learn to speak from the mother, then at the origin of this circle there is not one's disposition to speak as a function of some other. In the primary relationship with the mother, we have in mind exactly what the other had in mind, and before we were able to speak with the other, there was a time in which we spoke only with the mother, and only to reestablish the *originary common place.*

However, at this point it is not yet clear why the discovery of the principle of mediation, which is the very principle of our speaking, made me feel like a sailor who gets to a port after a difficult navigation. Didn't I speak before that discovery?

I did speak, but without a logical order. I oscillated without criteria between the conformity to given rules and the arrogance of speaking. Actually, I had a criterion regulating my communication. It was the aforementioned criterion according to which I could say everything as long as it was likely. I learned this at school, at my language school. It was a hard school, but it was not useless even in its own limited way, as anyone who reads me can judge. Now I can see how that pseudoprinciple of communication was an approximation of the principle of passing by way of what others also have in mind. Unlike the pseudoprinciple, this principle safeguards the truth value of my experience, which is an absolute value that the accepted necessity of mediation does not contradict. In fact, this necessity reinforces that value. According to this principle, which is the authentic motive force of the originary structure of knowledge, there are no limits to the sayable but only rules about what can be said. There is actually only one rule immanent to sayability itself, and that is to recognize the necessity of mediation.

But this is not enough to explain my joy. In need of mediation, I saw the actual movement of my coming into the world being renewed. Just as "life is itself for me" ("*A vida se me è,*" Clarice Lispector writes[12]), and it is received life, so my feeling and willing must be given to me—must be mediated—in order to become mine. By making me get out of myself, that principle has made me find my deepest inner self. That principle made me feel that the woman who gave me life meant also to give me the word. By bringing me into the world, she wanted and has always wanted my symbolic independence as a part or more than a part of the life she gave me. Indeed, this explains the aforementioned sense of happiness we have when we come ashore after a difficult navigation.

Through the density of my intuition—which I am obliged to dilute in order to explain it—I realized that language exercises the function of a mediator, and that consequently language agrees with the sayability of all my experience. In the coincidence of mediation and agreement, I saw language as a substitution that gave me back my oldest and most original experience: the experience of coming to life and into the world. (When I say language, besides language in the strict sense I also mean the codes depending on it.) I realized that language is for me the first one in the place of the mother, and in this function I saw that language is absolutely irreplaceable.

Peirce has divided the representational function of signs into three types: the indexical function (the sign is an indication or an index), the iconic function (the sign is an image), and the symbolic function (the sign is a norm for the interpretation of the real).[13] If this trichotomy can also be applied to the organized set of signs, that is to say language, then I could say that during the journey I have described, I have come to see language in relation to the mother in the triple mode of the index, the icon, and the symbol.

It cannot be denied that language is indexical in relation with the mother; this is also signaled by the attribute "maternal," which is given to the first language we learn, the words of which (and not other words) translate our experience. The way the mother teaches us to speak is as effective as the way we experience learning to speak a foreign language spoken by the person with whom we fall in love. In fact, love makes us experience again the symbolic availability that characterizes the couple creating the world.

The iconic relationship was very important during my journey. Many times I happened to write: "I have seen," which is not my usual way of thinking and expressing thought. At that moment, in language, I happened to see an icon of the mother's work of weaving life together.

Last, we have the symbolic relationship. According to Peirce, on whose theory I base my own, the nature of this relationship is normative. The meaning of a word is a law or a rule for interpreting the real: "A Symbol is a law, or regularity of the indefinite future."[14] As a matter of fact, the common place or the common means that takes shape through the linguistic exchange cannot be reduced, as we know, to a convention among speakers or to one of their productions. Once that common place or means is found, it becomes a bond to them and what the speakers have in common is the fact that first they all accept the normativity of language more than the knowledge, let's say, of the exact meaning of words. We have already said that when we speak to each other, the meaning of words exists and any dispute in regard to meaning is not in order for us to reach an agreement, but rather, to establish what the meaning in the language we speak is. We do that with an attitude in which the initial movement of speaking and the search for a point of view in common with the mother are reproduced.

Psychologists say that, at a certain point, the mother is no longer able to perceive by intuition exactly what her child's needs are. This is a reductive way to explain the story of the creating couple. What happens, instead, is that at a certain moment the mother *withdraws*—just as God's Kabbala explains the creation of the world—and the child [*creatura*] or, better, the part-being, then wants to go back to being part of the whole. This is somehow achieved by speaking.

We can see the normativity of language translating the authority of the mother also in the fact that the normativity is not exercised as a law but as a living (rather than an instituted) order. As a matter of fact, linguistic order is maintained not by strictly observing its rules but by means of its constant transformation that allows it to take shape again in spite of and even thanks to the countless irregularities of our speaking. Actually, the linguistic order is such that there is never a linguistic state that can be said to be disordered, or needing order to be restored. In other words, it is a creative order that includes us even when we do not understand it and when we do not understand each other.

These characteristics of language correspond to the most classical attributes of the might [*potenza*] of the mother; they are also often used in reference to God. The parallel language-mother, or the parallel language-mother-God, could be further examined, but we must ask ourselves what it is worth. What I said in reference to this parallel and specifically in relation to the iconic relationship between language and the work of the mother, which I united in the metaphor of weaving, may seem a metaphorical way of speaking. But speaking metaphorically does not correspond to what I mean. As I have already written, I am not speaking of the mother metaphorically. To me, the necessary substitution of the mother is not equivalent to her metaphorization.

The reason why I keep repeating this is obviously because I feel that the words I use when I talk about the mother take on a metaphorical meaning. But why?

A first answer can be found in what I wrote about the maternal continuum as a natural and at the same time a symbolic structure to which the daughter belongs. In traditional culture, the power of the mother has lacked and still lacks a female genealogy. In other words, it has lacked an appropriate way to express and to exercise itself. When there is no mighty mother-daughter relationship, it happens that the mother may become a metaphor for everything. As a matter of fact, the power of the mother is represented in monstrous form as the phallic mother.

Even if we recognize that the relationship with the mother cannot be substituted, it is not enough; we have to recognize its principal value, by which I mean the value of a principle. The way in which the circle mediate-immediate comes to operate to give a beginning to the word is a proof of that value. So our fixation on the mother stops being regarded as something pathological. Actually, that fixation stops becoming such, as it happens, on the contrary, that we become sick when our feeling does not find its symbolic translation.

It happens that women get sick because they do not know how to love the mother because they are hysterically attached to her, literally: from the inside and completely. As others before me have noticed, this shows that in our culture the hysterical body still represents today the greatest obstacle to the complete appropriation of the mother by men and their symbolic order or disorder.[15] It is precisely the experience of the hysterical body that I am trying to translate into knowledge.

It is important, then, that my discourse does not fall back on the metaphorical: it would only reproduce the necessity of female suffering. To what should my discourse be anchored? *Not* to the body, as some women have answered. It cannot be anchored to the body because this is the answer in force in our culture, for which women, at least some women, pay by suffering symbolic disorder and imprisonment within the law. In the following chapters I will have to go back to the problem of how to save female discourse from drifting into metaphor and of how to save the hysterical body from imprisonment within the law. That is, I will have to talk about politics.

Chapter Notes

Chapter 4, page 51: I am aware of the problem of calling "male" a culture to which women, including me in my small way, have also contributed more or less actively. I call it male on the basis of the criterion according to which the prevailing authority exercises its mediation, an act fundamental to every culture. A culture in which authority is by preference identified with being man is a male culture. It is a question of a symbolic criterion (authority is symbolic, otherwise it would not exist as such). The culture in which I am expressing myself at present is female. Men, like Plato or my father or my teacher of metaphysics, are also part of this female culture whose mediating authority is, then, female.

Chapter 4, page 56: The literature on hysteria is vast, and what I have read of it is comparatively little, though in itself it is quite a lot. I will just point out a few titles: Ilza Veith, *Hysteria: The History of a Disease* (Chicago: University of Chicago Press, 1965); J. Michelet, *La Sorcière: The Witch of the Middle Ages*, trans. L. J. Trotter (London: Simpkin, Marshall and Co., 1863), especially for the wellknown event of the Ursulines of Loudon (255–76); see also "La stoffa del sogno e il nostro divenire etico [Dream Fabric and Our Becoming Ethical]," *Centro documentazione donna di Firenze* (Florence: Quaderno di lavoro, 1989), n. 4. Freud wrote extensively about hysteria. I quote a long passage from his "Female Sexuality" (1931): "Everything in the sphere of this first attachment to the mother seemed to me difficult to grasp in analysis—so grey with age and shadowy and almost impossible to revivify—that it was as if it had succumbed to an especially inexorable repression. But perhaps I gained this impression because the women who were in analysis with me were able to cling to the very attachment to the father in which they had taken refuge from the early phase that was in question. It does indeed appear that women analysts . . . have been able to perceive these facts more easily and more clearly because they were helped in dealing with those under their treatment by the transference to a suitable mother-substitute. Nor have I succeeded in seeing my way through any case completely, and I shall therefore confine myself to reporting the most general findings and shall give only a few examples of the new ideas which I have arrived at. Among these is a suspicion that this phase of attachment to the mother is especially intimately related to the aetiology of hysteria, which is not surprising when we reflect that both the phase and the neurosis are characteristically feminine, and further, that in this dependence on the mother we have the germ of later paranoia in women" (*Standard Edition*, vol. 21: 226–27).

Chapter 4, page 57: The anecdote of a pupil of mine, who appealed to the authority of her mother to support her cosmological theory, raises the problem of the conflict between the authority constituting symbolic disorder and other instances like school manuals, current law, scientific societies, and so on. I think that in many cases this conflict can be advantageously avoided by appropriate mediations. For instance, in the case in question, we could say to this pupil that, in the language we speak, we call earth that which holds up our feet, and that this earth is also round (giving her proofs of that). Then we could introduce her to the current cosmological theory as a point of view with which many have agreed, at least for a few centuries.

Chapter 4, pages 60–61: Rereading the account of how I came upon the principle of mediation, I notice that I have disregarded an aspect that could better explain the feeling of relief I felt at that point. I felt liberated from my subjection to thousands of rules and the obligation to follow them that was as burdensome to me as my impulse not to follow them. I felt relieved not in a mystical sense, which implies going beyond the regime of mediation, but I felt relieved simply by having understood the purpose of mediation. When I wrote the story, as one can see from the text, I took it for granted that I would and should find new rules. Now I do not think that anymore. The context and the acknowledged necessity of mediation are enough to help me remain in the symbolic order of the mother. I practice the regime of mediation in the form of a personal bond. I am becoming increasingly convinced that outside this type of relationship there is nothing but the law.

Chapter 5

The Circle of Flesh

As I said earlier, generally speaking I accept the response of the classical philosophers when they argue for the necessity of thought in order to "save" the truth-value of experience. I learned this at my school of philosophy. In other words, I accept metaphysics. But I exclude from this that which aims to make the work of the mother superfluous and consequently to invalidate her authority. I add this stipulation (a real "clause"): for me, metaphysics is valid if it assures that what my mother has done for me and what she represented when I was a child in need of her cannot be obliterated or replaced.

It might seem strange that I insist on talking about metaphysics. In fact, what it is usually meant by this word corresponds to what my stipulation excludes in favor of the mother. Metaphysics is presently conceived as the positing of another world. On the contrary, since my stipulation does not recognize a point of view superior to that of the originary relationship with the mother, it excludes any possibility of redoubling the world of experience in another world. The real and true world is precisely the one into which my mother has brought me after nine months of gestation.

It is clear that what I mean by metaphysics does not correspond to the current notion. For me, metaphysics testifies to the necessity of thought so that being does not end up in nothingness. There is metaphysics in the simple fact that in order to say something we need to say something beyond what is given. There is also metaphysics in those arguments rejecting metaphysics, thus proving its necessity.

Ernst Mach wrote of an "impulse towards completion" of the facts that is present in us "like a power from without."[1] I believe, instead, that this impulse corresponds to a logical necessity expressed by the principle that there is no being without thinking (Gramsci).[2] But the mere attachment to the mother and to the life she has given us is not a solution to the problem of the sense of being; even from the point of view of my itinerary, this attachment must turn into knowing how to love her. Thinking is necessary in order for the present to be known to us; it is necessary to show forth—to de-monstrate [*di-mostrare*]—experience and to make being be [*far essere l'essere*]. These are all in different ways paradoxical formulations. But I do not know any other way to say what human beings do when they learn to speak and when they speak.

The de-monstration [*di-mostrazione*] of experience is the focus of the political practices of coming to consciousness: class consciousness of those who put themselves on the labor market, female consciousness-raising [*autocoscienza*], self-consciousness of those without defense from capital (I have coined this phrase but its meaning is evident). These practices have in common the characteristic of turning a first-person experience into self-knowledge and into a knowledge of the world. They carry out this transformation in the simplest way, that is, by a free physical meeting of people and by the exchange of words regulated by the will to understand and to make oneself understood. The feminist Emma Baeri, from Catania, has spoken of the "circle of flesh," felicitously blending together the idea of maternity with that of mediation in one expression.[3]

One could object that for women, for male and female workers, and for the poor of the three economic worlds, the necessity of mediation in order to know what they actually experience in the first person depends on historical conditions such as ignorance, fear, or deceit in which they are compelled to remain. Therefore, unlike the necessity of metaphysics, the necessity of mediation is not a logical necessity. Like the ducklings in Lorenz's experiment, which took the head of the scientist for their mother duck's head, we could say that the condition of women, workers, the poor, and so on is not normal.

But I wonder if I can separate reality from logic in this way in order to judge one on the basis of the other. My "clause" suggests that I cannot or at least I cannot completely do so. According to my stipulation, the mother cannot be subjected to a superior point of view. In terms more familiar to the history of philosophy, my stipulation says that the opposition between what is innate in us and what is acquired, between the biological and the cultural, the natural and the historical, and other oppositions related to them, has a limited validity. These oppositions are not valid from the viewpoint of coming to life and into the world. From this point of view, everything is innate, and everything is acquired. Our ability to speak cannot be explained otherwise. We learn to speak with the same difficulty and the same naturalness as we learn to walk or to put a spoon into our mouths.

Well, something like this can also be maintained about the opposition between the logical and the factual. There is a point of view in which logical necessity and factual necessity cease to oppose each other and are the same necessity. I have mentioned this point of view many times. It is the viewpoint of the relationship that creates the world, when the world is born together with us and with our learning to speak, and having sense coincides with being true.

By saying so I do not mean to efface the distinction between logic and factual reality; that would be absurd. Rather, I want to build a bridge between the two. Philosophy teaches us that there is a logical necessity (that of Pythagoras's theorem in Euclidian geometry, to be clear) and a factual necessity (for instance, that I am a woman and my youth is gone). The first type of necessity is a relaxation and a joy for the mind that grasps it. In contrast, factual necessity can be a hard test and can even end up being intolerable to the mind, which will reject it with an enormous expenditure of vital energies. The bridge between the two orders of necessity is established when I realize that accepting factual necessity is as logical as accepting logical necessity. Arriving at this conclusion gives us a joy and a relaxation that are far better than those given to us by the demonstration of Pythagoras's theorem. Surely whoever is reading me will not find it hard to understand the greater joy we feel when we recognize that accepting factual necessity is no less logical than accepting a logical deduction, although the two are far apart from each other. That is precisely the reason.

There you have it, this is what the happy intuition that ended the chapter on the gift of the word consists of. The bridge between logical necessity and factual reality gives birth to logical order. The fact, once accepted, becomes a principle that gives order to experience and frees the mind. The real frees itself from being trapped between the blind repetition of itself and becoming always other than itself [*sempre da altro sé*].

Although empiricism, prevailing for instance in psychology and in sociology, puts experience in the first place, this is not enough to save experience in the sense that I have mentioned. The reason empiricism is not enough is because in interpreting experience it uses ready-made mediations instead of those required by experience itself. For instance, according to psychology and sociology, the contradictions that gave rise to the politics of women—contradictions such as hysteria, frigidity, language inhibition, estrangement from politics—were nothing more than pathological phenomena that were variously interpreted but always from the point of view of a subject that was not inhibited, hysterical, or frigid. The value of experience, which is not only a truth-value but also a value of enjoyment, is safe only when the circle of mediation is complete and substitution becomes restoration.

The reason I bring up metaphysics, a cumbersome word with a cumbersome history, is precisely to prevent the circle of necessary mediation from enclosing itself in a round of conventional rules that would exclude from its interpretation live experience (my experience!) and the authority of the mother.

Our culture is becoming increasingly aware of the necessity of mediation; perhaps this is its main characteristic. In our culture we are becoming more aware that what we communicate to each other is a symbolic product, the result of a series of operations of codification and decodification, in which we participate less actively and less grandly than we imagine. Only naive people think that what words, images, and gestures come to signify is the direct expression of what one wants to say, ignoring the determining influence of cultural mediation. In reality, it is never an experience, never an intention in its pure state, but, on the contrary, it is always a culturally determined version of them, et cetera.

This way of thinking is not reducible to simply coming to see [*presa di visione*] things as they are. It is a coming to consciousness, and consequently, it interacts with its object. In fact, I see that it interacts in the sense of making it truer than it is. How? In many ways, for instance, creating intolerance toward those who speak naively, no matter what they say. In this way, awareness of how communication works tends to become an obligation situated above what we intend to say.

Some explicitly speak of an ethics of communication, putting contents and effectiveness on a second level. I recall a comment by an English-speaking friend of mine, a true feminist, who after having read Luce Irigaray's *Speculum* said that although new, and perhaps valid, the language was unbearable, dictatorial, and it lacked an ethics of communication.[4] So I began to reflect on the philosophical prose of English speakers, which I already found strangely opaque and complicated in comparison to their literature and poetry. Is the language of the mother still alive in art, whereas it is dead and embalmed when it is a matter of demonstrating the true? Is it perhaps because another authority, another symbolic order has taken over?

The rules of the first language we speak are born from a logical and at the same time factual necessity of mediation. In fact, they are the conditions set by the mother so that we can always go back to communicate with her, sharing her experience of the world. Later those rules become complicated because new interlocutors, new authorities, and new experiences take over. In particular, I am thinking of how, in the schoolteaching of language, the strictly linguistic norms intertwine with those of civic coexistence (in which children feel they are assigned a space and a time of learning) and with arbitrary impositions of established power (such as, for instance, the prohibition against speaking in dialects). The same happens to the rules of exchange within professional classes, traditions of thinking and society in general: these rules are a mixture of dissimilar instances too. Even those languages that we declare have the purpose of making communication easy, like the jargon of mass newspapers, propose once again a blend of necessary rules with others only supposed to be so, but that instead are more or less arbitrary conventions and impositions.

Perhaps it is inevitable that mediations that are logically necessary are blended together with those that answer to a different kind of necessity, such as, for instance, the necessity of maintaining a specific power. But the maternal language, strictly speaking—that is, the language that takes shape in the exchange between word and experience originally regulated by the mother—suffers as a consequence of this mixture. We must keep in mind that linguistic exchange cannot be reduced to an exchange among speakers. It is always also an exchange, more or less successful, but always somehow sought, between word and experience. This is its permanent origin and its resource of originality.

An ethics of communication and other operations of that kind take law into a sphere that by nature belongs to the symbolic order of the mother. This can commonly be observed in its effects of conformism of the word. The word separated from its matrix dries up. The exchange between word and context fails; the meaning of words is flattened by recourse to definitions; judgment criteria become uniform: gestures, together with any other nonverbal expression of the mind, disappear.

In this way the world of experience agreed on and sayable according to conventional rules takes over the world sayable according to the language of the mother. In saying this I do not maintain that the world expressed with the language of the mother is more beautiful and richer than the other; actually, it is sometimes the other way around. It is just that this world corresponds to the language that is alive. It can develop by itself, whereas the other world is fixed. It changes only if one has the power to manipulate its rules.

In the past, those who held the power had to have recourse to violent repression, like jails, asylums, censorship, or the stake, if they wanted to exclude something from what was sayable. Today, mere novelty, ignorance of some rule or obedience to other rules is enough to isolate what is truly new.

Besides, and this is the point I wanted to get at, the substitution of a conventional language for the maternal language leads us to forget that mediation is necessarily in relationship with what is *immediate.* Thus, the product of mediation takes the place of immediacy, and an absolute regime of mediation is formed. This regime claims to function independently from its limits, and it imposes this pseudo-independence as its absolute rule. The awareness of the necessity for mediation, which as I said characterizes our culture, has now flowed into this regime of mediation. Consequently, it is claimed that what we are talking about is no longer the world of experience but a world of words; that is, of ready-made mediations. This regime is the newest mask of established power, its postmodern mask.

In the Italian language a woman who teaches at school is called *maestra* [schoolmistress] or *professoressa* [lady professor], and a woman who works in a factory is called *operaia* [woman worker]. On the other hand, according to conventional language, a woman who is at the head of a government is called *il sindaco* [mayor] or *il primo ministro* [prime minister] or *il presidente* [president]. The use of masculine forms [TN: marked in Italian by the definite article *il* and the *o* ending] shows how sexual difference expressed in grammatical genders, as in many other symbolic forms from poetry to fashion, does not exist in itself. We see it because of the symbolic forms. In this way female experience, deprived of the possibility of signifying itself, finds itself completely consigned to the cultural codes in force and to those who have the power to manipulate them.[5]

Let it be clear that although I support those who are naive, I do not pretend to be so. I realize that the world I am talking about is a world that is already signified, a signified-world. But this does not mean that it hides the real world from us, because the two worlds, supposing we can call them so, between them make a circle, and this circle constitutes the true world. Taken separately, the signified world and the real world are nothing but abstractions, although there are ways of living and thinking that come close to these abstractions.

Through the practices of consciousness raising, we are led to discover that the true world is that which is given in our experience through the word and in the word through experience. For me, this discovery is equivalent to finding the viewpoint of origins when the world was born together with us and with our knowing how to speak. In the true world, the new can take place. This is its definition. In the world without the symbolic there is only blind repetition; in the world of the conventional symbolic only what was expected takes place.

The complete circle of mediation in which I am included body and soul, flesh and bone gives birth to the world. This big circle is alive, and it is not a utopia. Human beings are born and grow up in this circle. All we know of language, of thought, of mental health agrees with the thesis that the world in which life comes to be, to develop and to have a sense is a circle of body and word without any absolute priority of one or the other.

Certainly this is not a perfect circle and the circulation it creates is not perfect because this circle does not realize the coincidence of the immediate and the mediate. I believe that this missing coincidence leads us to substitute for this world other ideal worlds or the fictive world of convenient truths.

The stipulation I enunciated at the beginning of this chapter does not allow me to accept both solutions. My stipulation does not apply only to metaphysics. It also excludes the possibility of redoubling the world of experience in another world of a conventional nature. Like ideal worlds, conventional worlds also exhibit entities, laws, and operations created only to give the idea of having achieved a self-sufficient discourse. From this point of view, Wittgenstein's intellectual biography is instructive. Wittgenstein started with the intention of substituting for everyday language a language that is logically correct, but he came to the conclusion that everyday language knows very well what it does and does it well, too. It is well known that it was determining for Wittgenstein to observe how children learn to speak.[6]

Conventionalism is like a recurring scheme. We find it in almost every epoch and field of our culture, supporting different positions. All these positions have in common the supposition that between being and language there is a sort of mutual indifference. Conventionalism bases itself on the nihilism of fictive being that I mentioned earlier when I reflected on the authentic sense of being. Conventionalism finds support in nihilism in the sense that it represses being because those who truly exchange being for its fiction, those who confuse them, those who cannot tell what is said to be from what is, these people, often a child or a woman, tend to pretend immoderately, making fun of the conventional order with all its rules and its seriousness.

Hegel noticed this phenomenon in reference to women's position within the social and political order of men, and it inspired a famous page in the *Phenomenology of the Spirit*: "Womankind—the everlasting irony [in the life] of the community—changes by intrigue the universal end of the government into a private end."[7]

But most of the time this objective derision does not make women happy. To the female mind, conventionalism can be an escape (to imagine being a "person" instead of a woman is the fictive freedom and immortality available to every emancipated woman). But more often it is a trap. Rules allow us to agree with one another on the meaning of words, on the criteria to determine whether something has or does not have meaning, whether it is true or false, and so forth. If from those rules we remove our reason, which is our experience together with the necessity that our experience has to acquire sense, in the vacuum so constituted the pure power of making and changing the rules takes over. As a matter of fact, behind the rules on which we have agreed there is the power to make and change them, which operates in a manner that I can only call a trap (without ruling out other ways of saying it), because I do not know it otherwise.

To my way of thinking, which is also always feeling because of my attachment to the matrix of life, rules can be separated neither from their reason nor from the substance of life that comes to be regulated. Consequently, respecting the rules always to some extent has the characteristics of a loving act, whatever those rules are, including grammatical rules. On the contrary, law never expresses anything other than the impersonal necessity of its own existence, whereas its contents are always provisional and debatable. In this emptiness of the law it is as if the so-called hysterical woman, that is, the woman who does not know how and does not want to separate herself from the mother, falls into a trap because she takes the law for her mother, but later she discovers that it is an insensitive, distant, dead mother. I will never forget what I suffered when I found myself in that situation, and I did not want to or could not accept the pretended reality anymore. It was an agony, the awfulness of which was equaled only by the happiness I felt when I later discovered the principle of true mediation, which puts the substitutions for the mother in circulation with her restoration.[8]

Conventionalism does not create symbolic order for the same reason that an artificial language cannot take the place of a natural language. The so-called natural languages or mother tongues, the true languages, differ from artificial languages because their relationship of exchange with reality is alive: they are never indifferent to it. Natural languages change together with changing reality, and they participate in that change, how shall I say it, freely, or I should say they participate in that change in the same way that human beings do and along with them, actively and passively. The life of a language is made most clearly manifest to us by this change of which I am speaking. But even if we consider the most ordinary aspect of language, for instance, the way in which the sounds of vowels and consonants are arranged, even if we think of the so-called grammar and syntax, we can see how natural languages always answer in a fine and constant way to the demands of signification so that nothing of our experience is excluded, if possible, from the possibility of being expressed.

In the image of the circle of flesh there is the idea of a true whose sayability embodies the context in which it takes shape because it forms as people are born and learn to speak, and because it forms from the circle of body and word without any absolute priority of one over the other.

We must not confuse the contextual true with the relative true. It is true not in relation to but together with time, place, and so on.[9]

The true gives birth to and makes true what has assisted its generation. For instance, this can be found in those tales of discoveries and inventions in which it is not possible to separate casual circumstances from necessary conditions because everything seems to be drawn into the process leading to the result. Then abstraction follows. That is, that true comes to be translated into a code that introduces it into the order of repeatability characterizing correspondence-truth, according to which it is true that "snow is white" if and only if snow is white. (Note that even this was a discovery at the moment when for the first time we saw snow and said, or we said and saw, that snow is white.)

In brief, my idea of the true is that its sayability embodies its context in the same way that a plant lives in its habitat. But in our mind, this idea encounters an obstacle that, in a way, makes this idea seem impracticable. In the same way, communication would be impossible, and on other terms it would be useless. The meaning of words fortunately depends on the context only to a small degree. This allows us to communicate what we are interested in communicating regardless of the original circumstances of its sayability. The meaning of "snow is white" is perfectly clear even if our grandmother who made us discover it is dead and gone! Otherwise, it would be a useless strangeness.

The obstacle to the idea of a contextual true is constituted by commodification, a major characteristic in our society. What this means is simply that in our society it seems possible to exchange anything for anything. Consequently, it seems easy, easier than necessary, to overlook differences and to leave contexts out of consideration even in linguistic communication.

Our experience as speakers as well as the variety of languages and their historicity contradicts the prospect of universal equivalence. It is well known how many obstacles, to date insurmountable, have blocked efforts to set up a translating machine. In spite of this, the idea that what can be said can be separated from every context and that it can be universally translatable is made evident to us by the availability of a universal equivalent, money, and of a symbolic structure, the market, where everything that enters loses its peculiar characteristics and becomes a commodity for exchange.

Apparently, the market does with commodities what language does with our experience. The market makes commodities exchangeable with any other commodities in the same way that language makes it possible to communicate our experience. But from the viewpoint of exchange, the market is more powerful than language because, unlike language, it has a "universal mediator" at its disposal that annuls qualitative differences and spatial/temporal distances.

For this reason, in his justifiably renowned analysis of the genesis and essence of money, Marx wrote that it would be wrong to compare money with language, just as earlier he had rejected a similar comparison with blood because "Language does not transform ideas, so that the peculiarity of ideas is dissolved and their social character runs alongside them as a separate entity, like prices alongside commodities."[10] As a matter of fact, money is the social character of commodities, which is separated (abstracted) from commodities themselves, whereas the meaning of words, which can be considered the social character of our experience, does not subsist separately from our experience because of the circular relationship that unites experience with its signification.

A separation similar to the separation that money makes can be admitted with regard to words only when we can translate them from one language into another; that is, when words take the place of other words, supposing that they are perfectly translated, which as we know is impossible. With regard to this Marx made a profound observation: "Ideas which have first to be translated out of their mother tongue into a foreign language in order to circulate, in order to become exchangeable, offer a somewhat better analogy; but the analogy then lies not in language, but in the foreignness of language."[11] Money, then, can be compared to the perfect translatability of languages into one another, something that is not possible but that would be possible if the language we speak first, the language of the mother, which substitutes and restores our experience, *did not exist*.

I believe that money, a "foreign language," is in a relationship of rivalry with the mother tongue and tends to supplant it in its work of humanization of human beings.

Marx's writing on money amply confirms my thesis, although Marx does not even indirectly put it forward. Marx *sees* money do in its own way that which competes with language; that is, money converts blind dependence on people and on things into a relationship of exchange. He also sees the distorted effects of exchange based on money instead of on the word. For instance, he writes, "In exchange value, the social connection between persons is transformed into a social relation between things; personal capacity into objective wealth."[12] Later on he writes, "economists themselves say that people place in a thing (money) the faith which they do not place in each other . . . because that thing is an *objectified* relation between persons."[13]

Perhaps because he lacked a theory of language, Marx does not conclude that commodity exchange has taken the place of linguistic exchange and that this could be the original sin of the market. Consequently, Marx doesn't even have the idea that the decisive game for humanity is always played, perhaps, at the level of the symbolic order.

I have neither the training nor, at this point of my research, the opportunity to develop a critique of Marxism from this angle, but what I know about it seems to confirm my intuition. For instance, it is well known that Marxism associates the origin of universal abstract thought with the use of money. If we exclude the explanation of deterministic materialism, how can we explain that the real abstraction, according to which exchange value is separated from use value, turns into the abstraction of thought?[14]

An answer may be found in my hypothesis according to which the process of socialization based on learning to speak is supplanted by socialization connected to the use of money. Speaking does not give the same secure symbolic independence that money gives. Cash does not stutter, does not make slips of the tongue or grammatical errors, does not create misunderstandings. Money makes itself clear immediately . . .

Mothers and grandmothers know what happens when they start taking children with them on their daily shopping. When children see the commodities and the act of trade they begin demanding things with such an obstinate persistence that their mothers or grandmothers can hardly recognize their (grand)children. But children's demands for things cannot be explained as defects induced by consumerism. Actually it is the other way around. I think that those children introduced to the market grasp its symbolic function. They react to it by speaking the language of buyers, perhaps out of fear of being the commodities on sale or out of attraction toward money, this new way of communicating that is so easy and powerful. From what I have observed, it seems to me that this behavior is more common with boys than girls, who as we know learn to speak earlier and better than boys. As I see it, the symbolic arrangement of the maternal continuum favors them.

Let's consider again the first of the two comparisons given and later rejected by Marx: "To compare money with blood—the term circulation gave occasion for this—is about as correct as Menenius Agrippa's comparison between the patricians and the stomach . . . To compare money with language is not less erroneous."[15]

In the light of the hypothesis of rivalry and substitution of the mother tongue with money, both comparisons have a greater significance than Marx recognizes them to have. Even the comparison of blood circulation has a deeper meaning if we think of the relationship between the gestating child [*creatura*] and the mother. Even Menenius Agrippa's comparison, which is false and mystifying if we examine the context in which it was used, that is to hush up a class conflict, is less false (and even more mystifying) if we consider the most elementary context it evokes. This is the context of our being bodily dependent on others, first of all on the mother. This most elementary context is the level at which conflicts, even the most justified ones, frighten. Only at this level can we overcome the fear of even the most frightening conflicts.

Chapter Notes

Chapter 5, page 70: Often I use the term *subject* and the themes of the subject, but I ask myself if this notion is necessary for me. I do not think so. I seem to resort to it out of convenience, in order to make myself more easily understood. In saying this I do not mean to reject this notion. I only want to declare it no longer indispensable. It seems to me that the thought of sexual difference is moving in the opposite direction from the philosophy of the subject. We may say "sexuated subject" or "woman as subject;" but what results from this juxtaposition? Actually, does anything survive this juxtaposition? I am not sure. I ask myself if the juxtaposition of subject and sexual difference has not aimed from the very beginning to eliminate one of the terms; that is, the subject. Perhaps the subject is making way for another being, the "circle of flesh." I am being vague because I am trying to understand better. Outside philosophy, in the mystical tradition, there is a line of thinking oriented around what we can call the death of the "I," which is becoming more evident. I am thinking of the later Simone Weil, the most recent Bateson (*Angels Fear*), or the most recent Fachinelli (*La mente estatica*). Carla Lonzi (see above, chapter 4, note 10) also showed a strong interest in the study of mystical women. See Carla Lonzi, "Itinerario di Riflessioni" ["Itinerary of Reflections"] in *È già politica* [*It's Already Politics*] (Milano: Scritti di Rivolta Femminile, 1977), 13–50. This is so much more important to my thesis because we owe to Lonzi the introduction of the concept of sexual difference into women's philosophy.

See the Milan Women's Bookstore Collective, *Sexual Difference*, trans. Patricia Cicogna and Teresa de Lauretis (Bloomington: Indiana University Press, 1990), 38–39. Now I think that the extra-philosophical theme of the death of the "I" is cropping up in philosophy in response to the waning of the subject. Quite an unforgettable waning, I must say, if we think of the great importance the notion of the subject has (had) in women's political language. The first time I suspected the waning of the "I" was when I read in a left-wing newspaper that women would be one of the "new subjects" in politics. This clashes with the way women feel deep down about their coming into politics, which is not to emancipate ourselves: we feel ourselves to be ancient, very ancient.

Chapter 5, page 73: My discourse on the ethics of communication shows some uncertainty. Reading it again I sense some traces of the rebellious tendency, complementary to my submission to the law, that I knew before I found the principle of mediation (see chapter 4, "Or the One in Her Place"). This does not mean that the principle of mediation implies some kind of ethics of communication. It teaches us, instead, to recognize in it at least a surrogate of the symbolic order—disempowered, of course, of any attribute creating sense-being. Another trace of that rebellious tendency is my constant difficulty in being uniform in writing bibliographical notes. In general, everything that is compulsory in intellectual work weighs very heavily on me. My difficulty is like the difficulty Simone Weil had with cleaning her room regularly, as she herself admitted. *Quisquilie* [trifles], Totò [Italian actor] would say. Of course they are trifles, but certainly they are also minute signs of the tyranny of the law, which otherwise would not be recognized (see below, ch. 4, note 13, p. 113).

Chapter 5, page 74: Writing this chapter has been particularly hard, and now I know why. I developed the critique of conventionalism keeping in mind the idea that the necessary mediation necessarily requires the fixation of rules—an idea that, unfortunately, besides being wrong, led me to conventionalism despite myself. In fact, this mistake could be avoided if and only if we avoid the pseudonecessity of submitting to a system of rules. Regarding this pseudonecessity, the mistake I made is rather surprising if we consider that my reasoning on the symbolic order always keeps in mind the mother tongue that, as everyone knows, we can learn and teach without rules. However, this mistake can be explained by the fact that at the time I was engaged with other women in an attempt to create a female society on the basis of common rules. Our attempt failed, and thinking it over led us to look for a symbolic order without common rules. Is it possible? We need to keep searching. In the last (unwritten) chapter of this book, I was supposed to talk about love; but I did not feel I was up to the task of dealing with it. I wanted to talk about love because I tend to see two regulating powers in (logical and factual) *necessity* and in *love*. Where is the problem? To my way of thinking it is a question of freedom for those without established power. Their freedom cannot depend on rights or on knowing how to use the rules of the game to their advantage. This would be putting the cart before the horse.

CHAPTER 6

The Abyssal Distance

For many years, ever since I became an adult, all around me I have heard talk of the contrast between children's need for approval and an adult duty to think independently. I have to say that I have never thought particularly about this problem, and I almost did not want to hear about it either. Then one day, not long ago, something in me rose up against the commonplace of adult independence, and I took the opposite side, as if I had been debating this question for many years. In a sense, this is just how it went.

I did not protest on the outside. I can just say that from deep inside of me a new thought arose. I came to think that, in the first place, I do not want an adult independence of thought or of anything else because more than that, I want a correspondence between (my) thinking and (my) being. It is only in this correspondence that I feel good. Only then can I actually say I, me, and mine. Second, I came to think that the correspondence I am looking for begins for me in recognizing the insurmountable feeling of dependence I have inside me, and in accepting it in spite of what is usually taught. So, to conclude, having become capable of an independent thought, I find myself in a new combination of dependence and independence in which the latter grows stronger through acceptance of the former.

I could say that after a lifelong search, at last I found a fertile intermingling of dependence and independence without, however, reaching maturity myself. A child's feeling of dependence is still intact inside me, and, in general, I did not have to make psychological or moral progress to arrive at this conclusion. I must say that for that matter, I did not even have to make intellectual progress either. My new understanding constitutes the crux of this short book, and I understood it as a consequence of the new combination of dependence and independence.[1]

The change in question can be compared to the shift in power from a usurper or regent to the legitimate sovereign. The new combination of dependence and independence inherited en masse the place, substance, and energies that I once invested in a vicious circle. It has given birth to what we could call a virtuous circle. Before the new combination, there was everything, but it was all turned the wrong way, so to speak.

I had better stop at this point to reflect on how this shift in power takes place.

Women before me have carried out careful and balanced feminist investigations that resulted in justifiably refuting the idea of an opposition between dependence and autonomy according to which one excludes the other. In particular I am thinking of Evelyn Fox Keller's main chapter of *Reflections on Gender and Science*, titled "Dynamic Autonomy: Objects as Subjects." Keller shows how the excluding opposition between dependence and autonomy characterizes a static conception of autonomy that ends up establishing a definition of power in terms of domination; "henceforth, its legitimacy resides in the phallus."[2]

From a theoretical point of view, Evelyn Fox Keller wants to create a realistic ideal of psychological development, reconciling autonomy and dependence. In practice, she promotes the formation of an alternative to the current modes of socialization of men and women in order to distinguish power from domination and to redefine power "in terms of mutual interests and well-being rather than primarily in terms of conflict."[3]

I find the ideal Evelyn Fox Keller describes convincing and fascinating, and her purpose is undoubtedly noble. However, I am not satisfied with her discourse, in general, because it does not explain how the desired modification can be realized. Human inclination toward the true and the good is not an answer to the problem of the conflictual socialization of men and women. Although I agree with her answer and I consider it actually very widespread, I do not think it is enough to get us out of the vicious circles to which the very structure of necessary mediation exposes us.

Keller does not ignore that structure. While arguing about psychological development, she emphasizes very appropriately its "inevitably autocatalytic and cyclical nature," for which the same facts act both as cause and effect.[4] Nor does she ignore the fact that this circularity may function in the wrong way by subtracting being (causing what I call a vicious circle and what she calls a dilemma). In fact she describes very well a vicious circle into which mothers easily fall when they see how the power of the father attracts his sons and daughters, because "They react to this devaluation [of themselves, mothers] in ways that often exacerbate their dilemma." Keller explains that "the intrusive mother . . . is a role that many mothers unwittingly assume in reaction to their own felt powerlessness," and "The more intrusive the mother, the more attractive the intervention of paternal authority," and so on.[5]

This type of observation, which can be multiplied endlessly, shows how useless it is to criticize what exists with the purpose of changing it. What exists reproduces itself not because it is considered good but because a mechanism stronger than our intentions and criticism propels it, no matter how justified those intentions and criticisms are. The problem, then, is to break this mechanism of repetition. As long as this mechanism operates, it uses everything for its own benefit, including our yearning for the good and the true, and including our longing to be free of it.

It is neither a moral nor a psychological problem. It is a problem of symbolic order. If the authority of the mother has no place in the symbolic order we obey, the result is that the behavior of the mother will regularly be considered intrusive or, vice versa, yielding, or, more often, both intrusive and yielding at the same time. This is because in the absence of a recognized necessity, her authority has no standard for its exercise or its acceptance. Until we break the vicious circles of a certain symbolic order, which for women is rather a symbolic disorder, reality will continue to bet in favor of phallic power and of the rigid opposition between autonomy and dependence, which is what Evelyn Fox Keller denounces.

The greatest disorder, which casts doubt on the possibility of women's freedom, is ignorance, women's included, of a symbolic order of the mother. Many women imagine their mothers in exactly the same way that Aristotle and Plato depicted her in their cosmologies two thousand years ago. That is, the mother was represented as a formless power and/or an obtuse interpreter of established power.

Time does not have the power to change the symbolic order, though it does change material reality. I have come to the conclusion that time and the symbolic order are equal necessities in that both of them mediate, both of them make the real thinkable. Let's not forget that time is also an order; it is the order we give to our experience of becoming. Generally, changes need time. But this is not the case for those changes concerning the symbolic order because, on the contrary, they interrupt or suspend time. Therefore, to think of a gradual change of the symbolic order is no more than a way to avoid a change. In fact, at this level change is either produced in an instant, or it is not produced, not even in two thousand years.

It is not easy to understand the symbolic. It is positive because it gives us what is positive of our experience. But it is in this act of giving that the symbolic hides itself. Therefore, we must inevitably explain the symbolic by subtraction. The way I prefer to proceed is to subtract its psychological content. I came up with this idea when I presented to an audience of women the thesis that only gratitude toward the woman who brought us into the world gives a woman an authentic sense of herself. By "gratitude toward the mother" I do not mean a feeling that may or may not be there, but I mean the pure meaning of those words, which is present in my mind even if I don't recognize her or if I have hostile feelings toward her. So I realized that by subtracting the psychological content from a word that is apparently solely psychological, like *gratitude*, I was not performing a metalinguistic operation that aimed to consider what "gratitude to the mother" meant in the Italian language. In fact, I discovered that the word also had another reference at the level of symbolic order. Some women experienced this other reference in the form of a painful feeling of the loss of any feeling of gratitude toward the mother. In fact, in patriarchal societies like ours, many women suffer from that loss.[6]

Similarly, we can characterize the symbolic order by subtracting all ethicality and logicality from it. This does not mean that the symbolic order is immoral or illogical, as Europeans thought of cultures different from theirs when they came in contact with them, and about which they had no desire to learn. In general, the symbolic order cannot be judged because it precedes and prepares judgment. That is, it is the self-presentation of the real according to an autonomous order of self-presentation itself (and *not* according to an autonomous order of the real).

The "shift in power" I described above led me to think of a new combination of dependence and independence. This "shift in power" corresponds to a change in the symbolic order that, because of its characteristics, deserves to be called revolutionary. Perhaps all changes that are called revolutionary as a result of their radicality and acceleration are produced in this form of substitution of a "virtuous" circle for a vicious one.

Once again we must face the difficulty of distinguishing act and contents. To understand what a revolution is, we must not consider the symbolic order as limited to codes (such as the economic system, the political system, the law, etc.) which can be reconstructed and from which it is relatively easy, at least for those who do intellectual work, to take their distance and to plan their modification. We need to consider the symbolic order in its actuality, as the system of mediations on which I depend in order to say what I am saying and for what I am not able to say, and in general for all that I can say and I wish to say, and so on.[7]

It is at this level of determined/determining mediation, in which I am spoken/speaking, acted-on/acting, and so forth, that the symbolic order reproduces itself and can also change. It is the level of the necessity of mediation at which the absolute intent to say intertwines with the means of saying, the immediate with the mediate. So effects become causes, facts become principles. At this level, experience stops laying itself open to external interpretations, and it produces its own interpretation. The real stops appearing as mere effect and becomes a principle. In plain words, it is at this level that there is freedom, if there is freedom.

The question is: can we plan to change the symbolic order? It is certain that the symbolic order can change, since history shows us it can. But is it sensible to conceive of a politics of modification of the symbolic order based, as I am suggesting, on the politics of women?

I think so. Undoubtedly the symbolic order belongs to the deep structures of human reality that make us unknowingly be this way or that way. But I believe that this does not exclude the possibility that the symbolic order can be the object of a modifying intention.

The French historian Fernand Braudel promoted the idea of "unconscious history."[8] Following Marx and Levi-Strauss, Braudel suggests that besides current history there is a deeper and slower type of history. This is the history of unconscious forms of the social. Braudel adds that the distinction between the bright surface, which for him corresponds more or less to classical political history, and the murky depths, that is, the material and symbolic structures that make us be and speak as we are and as we speak, is difficult and aleatory. Moreover, according to Braudel, the slower and deeper history "is clearly visible more frequently than one would willingly admit."[9] Braudel makes an important observation for the understanding of our time. He observes that today, in fact, people's awareness of a slower and deeper history has grown so acute that we can speak of a revolution, which Braudel calls an intellectual revolution. This revolution consists in openly confronting the semi-obscurity of that deeper and slower history in order to give it an increasingly large place next to and to the detriment of current history.

Perhaps Braudel was thinking, first of all, of a revolution in the historians' way of thinking. But while I was reading Braudel I thought, instead, of the political movements that find their strength in coming to consciousness. Both ways of thinking of this revolution can be easily related to one another. The new way to understand the writing of history can correspond to a change in the way we make history. In both cases, the change consists in the fact that we have given a larger place to our awareness of the reality we are than to the representation of a reality through which we make it be this way or that. This also explains the agency [*protagonismo*] of those-without-established-power.

Braudel writes that to make room *next* to representation means in the first place to make room *to the detriment* of representation. But after all that is not what it ultimately means, because between the reality we are part of and the reality of our representations there is not necessarily a relationship of opposition that excludes one or the other. There could be, instead, a fertile correspondence, as for instance in artistic production, or in my new combination of dependence and independence. As a matter of fact, in Braudel's words I also read my symbolic revolution.

But why should the symbolic revolution be called political? The answer is easy, although it requires a remark. It is called political because it is political.[10] Whatever concerns the symbolic order is also part of politics because the social order depends, in part, on it. Without symbolic relevance, a material power, however great it may be, would have little importance. If this is not completely obvious, that is because the definition of politics is not neutral, and it can hide part of its interests. This confirms, after all, that politics is not indifferent to issues concerning the symbolic order. Indeed, we could say that the first political issue is the definition of politics.

In making this remark I do not mean to bring up the problem of the definition of politics, but actually the opposite. I mean that if we do not agree on the meaning of the word politics, very likely we do not agree on some substantial question. I recall a curious problem that preoccupied me some years ago. I asked myself: what is the relationship between the politics I do and the present politics of professional politicians? Why do we use the same word for things that are so different? It almost seemed to me a case of homonymy. Obviously, now I do not think that anymore. Someone might suggest that they are two different ways of conceiving politics. But I think a more reasonable view instead is that the great distance between the politics of professional politicians and mine corresponds to a political conflict regarding symbolic power, that is, power over the regime of mediation.

There is a contradiction within every regime of mediation that I must now try to formulate. In very general terms, it is the contradiction between presence that speaks for itself [*si dice da sé*] and the necessity of mediation. Therefore, the contradiction concerns the originary structure of knowledge [*sapere*] with its intertwining of experience and logic. Nonetheless, I prefer to explain that structure in the terms through which I experienced it.

My historical research on Guglielma's heresy (thirteenth-century Milan), which I did about ten years ago, suggested the simplest formulation of this contradiction.[11] Guglielma Boema meant something new to all women and men who came in touch with her. They interpreted what was new in her as the female incarnation of the Holy Spirit. After her death they established a church in her honor, which was headed by a woman, Sister Maifreda da Pirovano. Note that although Guglielma never accepted the interpretation that she was the female incarnation of the Holy Spirit, she remained friends with those who formulated it. The Roman Inquisition persecuted and destroyed the church that was built in honor of Guglielma, and it also publicly burned Guglielma's body, which had been buried in the cemetery of the Abbey of Chiaravalle in Milan. Aside from the records of the trial, nothing of Guglielma Boema or of that whole sequence of events is left, except a grotesquely distorted memory.

If we accept that the first task of Guglielma's followers was to protect her female grandeur, what was their mistake? Or was their mistake due perhaps to the fact that what was new about Guglielma was not translatable into socially acceptable terms? And should we not give the followers credit for having tried to translate it anyway?

Evelyn Fox Keller encountered a similar problem after she published a critical essay on latent sexism in science, as I read in an Italian interview. Some objected that her criticism concerned language and not content, as she believed. In answer to this objection, Keller examined some scientific theories and demonstrated that some contents originate from sexist assumptions. During the interview she explained, "I have done this work as a molecular biologist capable of showing and supporting my positions with adequate tools." But that did not help her. As a matter of fact, the reactions were rather harsh. She says, "I had never before experienced such anger directed at me as when I tried to present my work. What happened afterwards was that all doors were closed to me."[12]

In both Keller's and Guglielma's cases there is, on the one hand, an attempt to signify a female point of view, and, on the other hand, there are the rules socially established for the expression of what one wants to say. In both cases, Evelyn Fox Keller and Guglielma find the words to say what they want to express, but this ends up being unacceptable in spite of the efforts they made to make it acceptable. Sister Maifreda and her followers tried to promote the cult of Guglielma's sanctity by entering into an alliance with the powerful community of monks of Chiaravalle. One might object that this was only a cover-up instead of a true mediation, as, after all, the records of the trial show. It is probable that Keller's colleagues would say the same about her scientific rigor in demonstrating her epistemological (or political?) thesis. This undecidability reveals the contradiction.

Keller explains, "It is in the nature of scientific thinking, of the scientific community, to tolerate a certain degree of criticism. If you go beyond the limits, you are cast out." This is an important observation, but it must be rectified in the sense that what she says about the scientific community is also valid for any group or institution that has a mediating function, in other words, that makes culture. The bigger the social role of a specific group, the more valid the observation. Today science is a large, perhaps the largest, distributor of certainties, and this explains why the scientific community reacts against Keller, just as the medieval Church reacted against heretics.

This brings to light a characteristic of perhaps every regime of mediation, which is that its rules fulfill the requirements of communication-signification, and they *also* fulfill other social demands. Consequently, the question of sayability is always and also a question of symbolic order. I already mentioned this problem when I spoke of the logically necessary mediations that blend, perhaps inevitably, with necessities of another type.

If this is the case, we must think that the pure circularity of experience and logic does not constitute the originary structure of knowledge [*sapere*]. Sayability is thus a question of symbolic order that is historically determined. Sayability depends on the set of mediations provided by a given culture. What can be said, therefore, is a historical instance that cannot be distinguished from a logical instance. The language we speak proves that thinking is language and language is historically determined.

I believe that when Saussure spoke of the arbitrary nature of the linguistic sign, he grasped this aspect of mediation. That is, mediation is logically necessary but its forms are not. I wrote earlier that the circle of mediation is imperfect because it does not make the immediate coincide perfectly with the mediate. The idea I am presenting now is the same.

This leads us to conclude that, first of all, between experience and its signification, no matter how faithful, there is an abyssal distance, which does not mean that it is either big, or too big, or small, since it cannot be measured. It simply means that it cannot be filled. I discover that this is true precisely when the signification is faithful. Second, the imperfect circle of mediation brings up a problem concerning symbolic power, which is a political problem in the most everyday sense of the word.

In fact, who or what decides what is sayable, if experience and logic are not enough? What actually keeps alive or kills the circle of mediation that language in itself guarantees me? How are the historically determined forms of mediation connected to its logical necessity?

Several women thinkers have responded to the systematic isolation of their attempts at autonomous female thinking by trying to adapt as much as possible to the rules of communication-signification in force. I myself was moving in that direction when I came across Keller's case. In order to be granted more consideration, Keller was particularly careful to express her point of view following the rules in force, but this did not help, as it would be obvious if we thought about it. Actually, she was rejected even more harshly.

So I came to think that we must take the opposite direction, which does not mean that we should become estranged (with the result of marginalizing ourselves) but, instead, that we should make a new symbolic order necessary. I start from this simple thesis: thought is mediation and the social order is a set of mediations that are more or less coherent, but in any case functioning. If the experience of a woman is not a true point of view, if female grandeur is difficult to sustain, if female freedom is considered a luxury like having a second or a third car, the most effective response will consist in increasing the demands for truth, grandeur, and freedom to make the need for mediation larger and larger. Perhaps it is our self-moderation that makes the issue of women's freedom, and consequently women's autonomous way of thinking, superfluous to the social order. Superfluous, and therefore nil: thought and freedom, in fact, respond to the order of necessity.

In her short book *La lingua della nutrice*, Elisabetta Rasy has defined women's self-moderation, partly against and partly in favor of what I am saying, as a "fatal sense of proportions that has always been a very tenacious enemy of women's experience—and women's politics—of life."[13]

Based on my personal history and reasoning, I think that women's self-moderation is due to an unresolved conflict with the mother that makes the viewpoint of the originary relationship impracticable. Until I brought to light the aversion I felt for my mother and any other mother figure; until I realized the great love I felt for her together with my need for her approval and my fear of not obtaining it; until I solved this problem of the maternal principle of mediation, the vehemence of my intent to say what I wanted to say fell into a circle with the submission to the established rules, as I have already explained. I ended up saying only what seemed plausible, no matter whether it was true, made up, likely, or sincere, since all circumstances were made irrelevant by the iron constraint of the circle of self-moderation. For me as for others, what was present to me [*il presente-a-me*] became literally insignificant, although it was still present in the unhappy form of an experience without sense.

The real without the symbolic is less than nothing. This sounds like a paradox. As a matter of fact, this is another version of the necessity of making being be [*far essere l'essere*]. According to some philosophers, evil would be a nonbeing. Instead, I think that evil is being less than nothing, and we have less than nothing when there is a real but there is no symbolic. This situation corresponds to that of the child [*creatura*] who is separated from the mother and cannot find the originary common place she or he had with her. That is, the child is not able to speak if we regard speaking as a way of finding again the point of view the child used to share with the mother. Due to the abyssal distance between everything we want to say and the means of sayability, we would never be able to find that point of view again if there were not someone who asked us to speak and assured us they understand what we wanted to say.

A woman discovers the symbolic need for the mother when self-moderation ends. This is what I discovered when I began listening to the great number of desires and fears I had. They are so out of proportion with the means at our disposal (is this another abyssal distance, or is it the same one?) that we fall into the defenseless state of childhood and into the need for the mother.

But is it conceivable that we would let large demands, desires out of proportion, violent feelings—in other words imbalance and disproportion—break into our own lives if we were not already sure that we have a superior force to balance them? (*La sproporzione* [*Disproportion*] is the title of Bibi Tomasi's collection of stories about women's freedom.[14]) Aren't we in a vicious circle? As a matter of fact yes, we are; it is the circle of self-moderation. I believe that it is the very circle of self-moderation that the maternal principle can break. What I mean is that the superiority of the mother and the necessity of her translation into a symbolic authority must be recognized in principle.

Earlier I asked myself: who or what decides what can be said if logic and experience are not enough? We must recognize that from the truth-confirming [*veritativo*] point of view there are no instances equal to logic and experience. It is just that they are not enough. On the one hand, experience in a pure state does not take place, and in any case it requires de-monstration and re-presentation. On the other hand, the mode of mediation is historically determined. Languages, scientific societies, churches, radio stations, television, newspapers, and even school principals, editors, and so on, are a series of instances that in many aspects can be considered contingent but that as such are never completely so, because mediation is necessary even between me and myself, and the abyssal distance passes through me, dividing me into two parts. I am not thinking of soul/body, although in the past this duality was a way to smooth over the problem. I am divided in every fiber and cell of my organism by the very regime of mediation: by its necessity and its inadequacy, which are inseparable, like the jaws of pincers we cannot escape. Except for the fact that we know it, and we explain it.

I began this symbolic operation of explaining the regime of mediation by saying that I neither brought myself into the world nor did I teach myself to speak. This led me to find once again the originary relationship with the mother.

Therefore, when I am asked who or what decides what can be said, I answer that in the first place it is the authority of the mother. The mother tongue, first mediator and first code, is proof of this. Scientific communities, parliaments, courts, markets, and other social institutions of the same kind, including my school of philosophy where they taught metaphysics, are valid instances, but they are secondary. They come after the mother.

This takes us back to my "clause" about the primacy of the mother, which shows us that it is enough to respect her in order to create a symbolic order in a historically given reality, whatever reality one might find oneself in. The maternal principle builds a bridge over the abyssal distance between the logical necessity of mediation and its historical forms, which can always be modified and in an unquantifiable sense are always arbitrary. I do not put the principle of the mother outside history: my history begins with the relationship with my mother. But I place it above authorities and powers whose codes make up both the symbolic and social order, any historical order in which one happens to live, we might say by chance if it were not for the history of our birth.[15]

This discourse has two distinct but inseparable levels. At a more accessible level, which is not evident yet (although the politics of women is emphasizing it more and more), there is an alternative and there is a choice to be made. We must choose whether we want to identify symbolic authority with established power, since it assures (or in the case of the established opposition it promises to assure) some kind of social synthesis, or whether we want to acknowledge the authority of the woman who brought us into the world and taught us to speak. It is because of our relationship with her that the mother is entitled to authority that, instead, established powers usurp from her, as Keller's case shows when the scientific society did not allow her to build a bridge between being a scientist and being a woman.

The word *usurp* shows that my choice is in favor of the symbolic authority of the mother. However, at this level the term could be excessive. In fact, at this level there is a choice and those who choose to grant symbolic authority to established power, which assures a social synthesis (on its own terms, of course), will not speak of usurpation but instead they will talk about substitution, and they will argue that after childhood we must learn to do without the mother. To my way of thinking, we do not have to, but we can do without her. Undeniably there is a symbolic order that is not that of the mother. I have chosen to substitute for childhood attachment to the mother knowing how to love her, and I have chosen to consider the language I learned from her as the first (archetypal) form of that knowing. I know of other women and men who have made this choice. On the other hand, yet other women and men prefer to substitute for the attachment to the mother an obligation within the regime of mediation, devoting themselves completely to their labor, to the state, to their family, to their religion, and so forth. They prefer languages they learned later, or artificial languages, or money, to the language of the mother. This can also be a choice.

At a deeper but very common level, there is no choice. At this level there is a female, and not only female, experience, the signification of which does not find in the given symbolic and also social order either a meaningful, a supportive, or a rejecting interaction, but only fortuitous reactions that can cause chaos or, if you prefer, hell. A frightening example of the lack of meaningful interaction between female experience and codified culture can be found in the history of the persecution of witches, which remains unexplained although extensive historical research has been done about it.[16]

There is the social body, which finds some kind of synthesis, and there is the wild body. I give this name to that part of human experience that goes beyond what a given symbolic-social order can mediate and that, consequently, remains outside of the social synthesis or enters into it as object of interpretation and of other people's interventions. Before the politics of women, female experience was this wild body.

I believe that for the type of human experience that is outside the social order, or is unhappily within it, there is only one possible symbolic order. This is the symbolic order that can refer experience to the authority of the mother. As a matter of fact, the authority of the mother represents the principle that has in itself the greatest capacity for mediation because it is able to put into the circle of mediation both our being body [*essere corpo*] and our being word [*essere parola*]. It is able to do this on this earth and not in heaven as, according to Christian promises, God will do at the end of time.

At this level, which is determining for the creation of the symbolic, there is no choice, but an inevitable struggle. For instance, there is struggle against the position of those who believe or want others to believe that there is choice even when there is not one—this is called pluralism. We must fight to prevent the social synthesis of established power from substituting for the maternal principle. We must give a social translation to maternal power in order to prevent social synthesis from closing up. We must fight to keep social synthesis open to anything we want to say, however distant or abnormal that may be.

For me, keeping the social synthesis open is the condition of freedom. Private property and rights are secondary conditions of freedom. They conform to historical syntheses that do not include me, just as they do not include most of female and part of male humanity.

Chapter Note

Chapter 6, page 87: I ended note 1 by saying "not beyond the necessity of mediation." Now I want to add that this necessity is not a form of slavery. The necessity of mediation is due to the fact that we live, symbolically, a life received, and our being, once again symbolically speaking, is given to us. The virtuous circle of freedom reproduces this structure; on the other hand, the vicious circle, which Keller calls a dilemma, reproduces this structure in the opposite direction. The circular shapes of Dante's Hell, Purgatory and Paradise express the notion of necessary mediation and of the two opposite directions according to which mediation can develop.

Notes

Chapter 1

1. G. W. F. Hegel, *Encyclopedia of the Philosophical Sciences in Outline*, ed. Ernst Behler (New York: Continuum, 1990), 48.

2. G. W. F. Hegel, *Science of Logic*, trans. A. V. Miller (Atlantic Highlands, NJ: Humanities Press, 1969), 67–68.

3. Descartes, *Meditations on First Philosophy* in *Selected Philosophical Writings*, trans. John Cottingham, Robert Stoothoff, and Dugald Murdoch (Cambridge: Cambridge University Press, 1988), 76.

4. Edmund Husserl, *The Crisis of European Sciences*, trans. David Carr (Evanston: Northwestern University Press, 1970), 151.

5. I use F. Sartori's translation of the Republic in *Platone: Opere* [*Plato: Works*] (Bari: Laterza, 1966). The translation of Descartes is mine [Muraro's], *Oeuvres* (Paris: Charles Adam and Paul Tannery, n.d.). [Translator's note: we cite from Plato, *Republic*, trans. Francis McDonald Cornford (Oxford: Oxford University Press, 1941), 227.]

6. Plato, op. cit., 521; 237 and 525; 242, translation modified.

7. Descartes, op. cit., 79.

8. Husserl, op. cit., 148–52.

9. Husserl, op. cit., 152.

10. Plato, op. cit., 539 b–c; 261.

11. Ibid., 540 c–d; 262.

12. Ibid.

13. Freud, *New Introductory Lectures on Psychoanalysis, Standard Edition of the Complete Psychological Works*, vol. 22 (London: Hogarth Press, 1964), 121. In reference to Freud's passage on the change-over [*conversione*] of the little girl (and of the woman) to the father (to man), Luce Irigaray writes, "this operation—and we can quote Freud's own words against him here—in no way constitutes a *displacement* of the origin-desire of the little girl, of the woman. It is more in the nature of an exile, an extradition, an ex-matriation, from his/her economy of desire. And she is actually held responsible for it:

does she not hate her mother? What really occurs, of course, is that the representation, the signifier of one stage in woman's libidinal economy (and not the least important stage since it is the one in which she was perhaps marked off from her first stage by her re-mark) is proscribed." *Speculum of the Other Woman*, trans. Gillian C. Gill (Ithaca, NY: Cornell University Press, 1985), 43. I agree with Luce Irigaray that the "hate" for the mother is just the consequence of a failure of symbolic elaboration of the old relationship with the mother. To a woman, this lack of elaboration is the cause of chaos, which Freud now interprets in terms of the social instead of the symbolic order. At this point, it seems appropriate to me to point out that later on Freud clearly realized that our civilization ignores or underestimates the importance that the little girl's love for her mother has in a woman's life. I am referring especially to what Freud writes in "Female Sexuality" (1931): "I was struck, above all, by two facts. The first was that where the woman's attachment to her father was particularly intense, analysis showed that it had been preceded by a phase of exclusive attachment to her mother which had been equally intense and passionate. Except for the change of her love-object, the second phase had scarcely added any new feature to her erotic life. Her primary relation to her mother had been built up in a very rich and many-sided manner. The second fact taught me that the *duration* of this attachment had also been greatly underestimated. In several cases it lasted until well into the fourth year—in one case into the fifth year—so that it covered by far the longer part of the period of early sexual efflorescence. Indeed, we had to reckon with the possibility that a number of women remain arrested in their original attachment to their mother and never achieve a true changeover towards men." I think and later on I will try to justify the idea that there is no "necessity" for any woman to make that change. It is rather a free option from Freud's point of view of the symbolic order (the "necessary change" is a loss in the logic of social order). Freud goes on to write: "This being so, the pre-Oedipus phase in women gains an importance which we have not attributed to it hitherto." Then Freud makes the well-known comparison with what, at the time, was a recent archeological discovery of Minoan-Mycenaean civilization: "Our insight into this early, pre-Oedipus, phase in girls comes to us as a surprise, like the discovery, in another field, of the Minoan-Mycenaean civilization behind the civilization of Greece" (*Standard Edition*, vol. 21, 225–26). A year ago when I gave a lecture in a refresher course for teachers I spoke of the "early relationship" with the mother and one of the teachers asked why I did not call that relationship archaic. I did not know then, and I tried to understand why I called it that. I answered her that perhaps I called it "early" by opposition to "modern," since for a woman to turn her back on her mother is the modern way. Now I think that my choice of the word *early* instead of *archaic* also comes from "the early pre-oedipal phase" that Freud talks about in his aforementioned passage.

Chapter 2

1. Adrienne Rich takes the metaphor of giving birth to oneself from a feminist poster: "Metaphors of midwifery and childbirth recur in the literature of the contemporary women's movement: a feminist poster bears the inscription, *I am a woman giving birth to myself,*" Adrienne Rich, *Of Woman Born* (New York: W. W. Norton & Company, 1986), 156. Rich connects this metaphor with the experience of childbirth. In this way, the metaphorization finds itself intercepted, as it were, by a realistic element. Is the result of this metaphorization comparable to my refusal to make a metaphor of maternal work? Yes, to the extent it makes us see our every action, including childbirth itself, as a completion of birth. In such a case the idea of redoing the work of the mother would fail. Considering the so-called Oedipus complex, Luce Irigaray adopts the same metaphor. Irigaray writes that perhaps man kills his father not out of a desire to take his father's place but because he wants to suppress the one who artificially cut his bond with the mother in order to take possession of the whole power of creation. Irigaray writes that in this case, "phallic erection, far from being allpowerful, would be the masculine version of the umbilical cord (. . .) a return to the world that allows them to become sexual adults capable of eroticism and reciprocity in the flesh." Then Irigaray writes, "This return to the world is also necessary for women" (*Sexes and Genealogies*, 17).

2. The stereotyped but unsuperseded opposition between idealism and materialism supports the idea that the maternal work, which consists in making our living body and in teaching us to speak, is presumably reversible and reproducible. I insist that these two operations are determining, unique, irreversible, and impossible to separate from her. Mentally and technologically we can unmake and remake everything except our being as a living body and our mother tongue. Without our body and our mother tongue, there is nothing we can begin to do. The simplest critique to all philosophies based on the notion of foundation-beginning consists in pointing out that when we think, we speak the historical language we have learned. Alessandro Manzoni criticized Descartes and his followers for not taking into consideration the fact that human beings "learn from others what you want them to discover by themselves; that they receive from others—by *means that not only they have not made up, and could not make up, but that they are not able even to use if they were alone*—what you want to make spring up absolutely from the small corner of their intelligence that the system leaves to them or removes from them." I stress that the word *means* corresponds, of course, to language; Manzoni quoted in Lia Formigari, *L'esperienza e il segno* [*Experience and Sign*] (Rome: Editori Riuniti, 1990), 203.

3. Some American feminists have made of poststructuralist critical thought the theory, perhaps the best theory, of feminism. Joan W. Scott

writes, "We need theory that can analyze the workings of patriarchy in all its manifestations—ideological, institutional, organizational, subjective—accounting not only for continuities but also for change over time. We need theory that will let us think in terms of pluralities and diversities rather than of unities and universals. We need theory that will break the conceptual hold, at least, of those long traditions of (Western) philosophy that have systematically and repeatedly construed the world hierarchically in terms of masculine universals and feminine specificities. We need theory that will enable us to articulate alternative ways of thinking about (and thus acting upon) gender without either simply reversing the old hierarchies or confirming them. And we need theory that will be useful and relevant for political practice." The author then goes on to say that according to her, "the body of theory referred to as poststructuralism best meets all these requirements." Joan W. Scott, "Deconstructing Equality-Versus-Difference: Or the Uses of Poststructuralist Theory for Feminism," *Conflicts in Feminism*, eds. Marianne Hirsch and Evelyn Fox Keller (New York and London: Routledge, 1990), 134. This is an example of intellectualism. How could the author think that a complex of theories elaborated in contexts, with interests, and for purposes foreign, if not contrary, to women's search for free social existence, could be the theory women need? In general, how could the author think, in light of poststructuralist thought, that a theory could be formulated independently from social and political practices, which should then put it on like a hat? Teresa de Lauretis critiques and corrects this intellectualism in her "The Essence of the Triangle or, Taking the Risk of Essentialism Seriously: Feminist Theory in Italy, the U.S., and Britain," *Differences: A Journal of Feminist Cultural Studies* 1 (1989): 3–37.

    4. Immanuel Kant, *Prolegomena*, trans. Ernest Belfort Bax (London: George Bell and Sons, 1909), 99–107. I draw the parallel between "mother" and "thing in itself" from J. Lacan, *Seminar Book VII, The Ethics of Psychoanalysis*, trans. Dennis Porter (New York: W. W. Norton, 1992).

    5. Immanuel Kant, *Critique of Pure Reason*, trans. Norman Kemp Smith (New York: St. Martin's, 1929), 258.

    6. Rich, op. cit., 224.

    7. Rich, op. cit., 225. The passages quoted are from the chapter "Motherhood and Daughterhood" where the author writes, "This is the core of my book" (118). Then Rich writes, "It is hard to write about my mother. Whatever I do write, it is my story I am telling, my version of the past. If she were to tell her own story, other landscapes would be revealed. But in my landscape or hers, there would be old, smoldering patches of deep-burning anger" (221). This supports my thesis that there is a mental trend of aversion toward the mother that can be found in the stories of many women. Further

on Rich writes about "the obscure lashings of feeling" that correspond to the symbolic disorder of which I am speaking.

8. The main sources for what I write on the sense of being are: Martin Heidegger, *Being and Time*, trans. Joan Stambaugh (Albany: SUNY Press, 1996); Edith Stein, "Martin Heidegger's Existential Philosophy," trans. Mette Lebech, *Maynooth Philosophical Papers* 4 (2007), 55–98; Emanuele Severino, "Ritornare a Parmenide," *Rivista di filosofia neo-scolastica* n.v. (1964): 137–75; G. Bontadini, "Sozein tà fainómena. A Emanuele Severino," *Conversazioni di Metafisica*, 2 vols. (Milan, Italy: Vita e Pensiero, 1971), vol. 2, 136–66. The question of the sense of being is difficult because it is elementary. Before raising the question of true/false, just/unjust, useful/harmful, and so on, there is the question of making or not making sense and how things acquire, lose, or change sense. The sense of things depends on cultural codes which, however, change. How? By chance? It is obvious that we cannot compare, for instance, different moral (or aesthetic, etc.) judgments if they are passed on the basis of different cultural codes. The same is valid for the question true/false. To say that the sun revolves around the earth is not false according to a specific meaning of "revolving around" and of being true/false. On the other hand, to decide or to accept that it is not true that the sun revolves around the earth is not merely an effect of a change of codes. It is also its cause. If we affirm that the earth revolves around the sun, we change the way of looking at reality. Therefore, we are dealing with a change that cannot take place if it has not already taken place. In other words, Copernicus's theory is both effect and cause of a change of cultural codes. Then, consequently, within the historical process we know as the Copernican revolution there is a point at which making sense and being true coincide. At this point I'd like to quote a motto by Charles S. Peirce: "It is not metaphysics that we are dealing with: only logic." The passage quoted is in *Collected Papers of Charles Sanders Peirce*, eds. Charles Hartshorne and Paul Weiss, 7 vols. (Cambridge: Harvard University Press, 1932), vol. 2, 44.

9. To be honest I do not have sure data to state with certainty that Freud coined the word "metapsychology" from "metaphysics." Metapsychology seems to be the first name that Freud gave to what later will be called psychoanalysis. In 1898 Freud wrote to Fliess, "I am going to ask you seriously, by the way, whether I may use the name metapsychology for my psychology that leads beyond consciousness." Jeffrey Moussaieff Masson, ed. and trans., *The Complete Letters of Sigmund Freud to Wilhelm Fliess* (Cambridge, MA: Harvard University Press, 1985), 301–2. On the other hand, it is known that the word "metaphysics" probably comes from the chronological order of Aristotle's books; in other words, the books on metaphysics come after (*meta*) those on physics. Therefore, it is important to note that the word was originally coined

metonymically and this is a mark of context on meaning. In the same way, in order to explain the sense of knowing how to love the mother, I resort to metaphysics. This is (also) because metaphysics was taught in my philosophy school. My way of speaking carries this biographical stamp.

10. In his "Autobiographical Notes" Einstein writes, "It was Ernst Mach who, in his *History of Mechanics*, upset this dogmatic faith [in mechanics as a base acquired from physics]; this book exercised a profound influence upon me in this regard while I was a student. I see Mach's greatness in his incorruptible skepticism and independence; in my younger years, however, Mach's epistemological position also influenced me very greatly, a position that today appears to me to be essentially untenable. For he did not place in the correct light the essentially constructive and speculative nature of all thinking and more especially of scientific thinking; in consequence, he condemned theory precisely at those points where its constructive-speculative character comes to light unmistakably." P. A. Schilpp, ed., *Albert Einstein: Autobiographical Notes* (La Salle, IL: Open Court, 1979), 19–21. In fact, E. Mach's intention, later taken up by the Vienna Circle, was to eliminate metaphysics from science.

11. Antonio Gramsci writes, "Without humanity what would the reality of the universe mean? The whole of science is bound to needs, to life, to the activity of humanity. Without humanity's activity, which creates all, even scientific, values, what would 'objectivity' be? A chaos, i.e. nothing, a void, if one can indeed say that, because in reality, if one imagines that humanity does not exist, one cannot imagine language and thought. For the philosophy of praxis, being cannot be separated from thinking . . ." A. Gramsci, *Further Selections from the Prison Notebooks*, trans. Derek Boothman (Minneapolis: University of Minnesota Press, 1995), 292. In his argument against N. Bukharin, author of *Theory of Historical Materialism: A Popular Manual of Marxist Sociology*, Gramsci attacks the idea that the real is supposedly independent of thinking (see Gramsci, *Selections from the Prison Notebooks*, trans. Quintin Hoare and Geoffrey Newell Smith [New York: International Publishers, 1971], 440–48). From Gramsci I learned to conceive of philosophy in terms of a bridge between "physics" and metaphysics (although Gramsci's use of language is different from mine). His philosophy contains a great number of concepts of extra-philosophical origin that he *introduces* into philosophy, in the same way that I am introducing into philosophy the notion of knowing how to love the mother. For Gramsci, philosophy does not need to create its own space among or above others. On the contrary, philosophy must encourage in every field the disposition to speak and to act in terms of the sayability of the true; that is, of the symbolic order. I take the notion of the "introduced concept" not from Gramsci but from Bontadini, who rediscovers in the Jewish-Christian tradition the concept of creation that he introduces into philosophy in order to resolve the contradiction of becoming. Bontadini

writes, "it is a question of an analogical, symbolic concept, precisely of an 'introduced' concept that is therefore surrounded by a halo of darkness, yet it is a concept we cannot give up" (op. cit., 145). On the other hand, we could say that Gramsci "introduces" into philosophy the whole of history together with a great number of extra-philosophical concepts.

12. Bontadini, op. cit., 145. In my judgment, his main text is "Per una teoria fondamento [For a Theory of Foundation]," *Metafisica e deellenizzazione* (Milan, Italy: Vita e Pensiero, 1975), 3–34. Bontadini argues with what Severino writes in his "Ritornare a Parmenide," op. cit. Bontadini states that "In reality *Parmenides is present in Plato and in Aristotle* (. . .) because (we must repeat) without Parmenides we could not explain the historical movement of metaphysical thought. Plato's doctrine of *chora* and Aristotle's doctrine of *hylé* reveal the presence of Parmenides too, since a true empiricist does not need such 'introductions' in the attempt to account for the irrational" (op. cit., 146.) To explain how Bontadini and I differ, I could say that I introduce the idea of an unthought and an unthinkable into classical philosophy; that is, the notion of a *tangible transcendent* (which I take from Luce Irigaray). In her last "London Notes," Simone Weil presents this concept with intuitive words and images; I will use them to expound that concept. The philosopher recalls an Irish story that tells of a woman whose young brother is sentenced to death. After witnessing his execution, she goes back home and in a vital reaction to his death she eats a whole jar of strawberry jam. Then, for the rest of her life she cannot stand to hear the words *strawberry jam* mentioned. Simone Weil comments, "It is only real feelings that possess this power of transferring themselves into inert matter. For living man here below, in this world, sensible matter—that is to say, inert matter and flesh—is like a filter or sieve; it is the universal test of what is real in thought, and this applies to the entire domain of thought without exception. Matter is our infallible judge." Then Weil talks about "this alliance between matter and real feelings" from which comes "the significance of meals on solemn occasions, at festivals and family or friendly reunions (. . .). And the significance of special dishes: Christmas turkey and *marrons glacés*," and so forth. Simone Weil concludes by saying that "the joy and the spiritual significance of the feast is situated *within* the special delicacy associated with the feast." (Simone Weil, *First and Last Notebooks* [New York: Oxford University Press, 1970], 363–64.) To my way of thinking, the concept of "tangible transcendent" means the primordial place that the relationship with the mother has before [*al di qua*] the physical/psychic, matter/idea. Therefore, this concept of tangible transcendent aims to overcome the opposition, nowadays sterile though still in use, between idealism (or spiritualism) and materialism.

13. What I write here on speculative mystics is based on what I read by William of Saint-Thierry, Hadewijch of Antwerp, Marguerite Porete, Meister

Eckhart, and from the anthology *Scrittrici mistiche italiane* [*Italian Mystical Women Writers*], Giovanni Pozzi and Claudio Leonardi, eds. (Genoa, Italy: Marietti, 1988). When we talk about mystical experience, in my opinion, we can and must also speak of experience in a rigorous philosophical sense. This requires a rethinking of our philosophical-scientific tradition both from a conceptual point of view (as Gregory Bateson and Fritjof Capra have begun to do, and as Elvio Fachinelli has also begun to do in his book *La mente estatica* [*The Ecstatic Mind*] [Milan, Italy: Adelphi, 1989]), and from the point of view of what counts and has authority in that tradition, as I would like to do in my small way—but with a major intent. That is, I would like to rewrite the history of philosophy in such a way that women's thought of their own experience would become part of it. As Clarice Lispector says so well, "the whole world will have to change for me to fit into it" (Clarice Lispector, *The Passion According to G.H.*, trans. Ronald W. Sousa [Minneapolis: University of Minnesota Press, 1988], 3).

14. Severino, op. cit., 137.

15. H. Kelsen, *General Theory of Law and State*, trans. Anders Wedberg (New York: Russell & Russell, 1961), 419. Kelsen writes at length on lack of confidence: "Only because man evidently lacks full confidence in his own senses and his own reason is he restless in his self-created and self-arranged world of knowledge. Only this undervaluation of his own self induces him to consider the world this self recognizes as a mere fragment, an inferior seedling of another world . . . Nothing is more problematic than the attempt to explain that which is given by that which is not, the comprehensible by the incomprehensible. And no less paradoxical is the psychological background of this epistemological situation: a diminished sense of self allows the function of the human spirit to degenerate into a merely dependent, and not at all creative, copying" (419–20). We could speak ironically about Kelsen's complaint as that of an undervalued male, bourgeois, Western "ego." I think that Kelsen's explanation is not false, but it is incomplete.

16. Translator's note: Descartes, op. cit., 96.

17. G. Bontadini, "La Deviazione metafisica all'inizio della filosofia moderna" ["Metaphysical Deviation at the Beginning of Modern Philosophy"], *Metafisica e deellenizzazione*, 45.

18. Severino, op. cit., 143: "Ontology sets out from a being that has lost its virility, which 'has loosened its ties' with being (. . .); it sets out from a positive that is negative, and since it has become dulled to the sense of being, ontology sets to work to find what it has not known how to discover by itself."

19. Lispector, op. cit., 3–4.

20. Lispector, op. cit., 173.

21. Lispector, op. cit., 170. It would be enlightening to compare these passages from *The Passion according to G.H.* (together with the mystical cul-

ture that appears through it) with what Charles S. Peirce writes about the category of Originality. "Let us now consider what could appear as being in the present instant were it utterly cut off from past and future. We can only guess; for nothing is more occult than the absolute present. There plainly could be no action (. . .). There might be a sort of consciousness, or feeling, with no self; and this feeling might have its tone (. . .). The world would be reduced to a quality of unanalyzed feeling. Here would be an utter absence of binary. I cannot call it unity; for even unity supposes plurality. I may call its form Firstness, Orience, or Originality. It would be something *which is what it is without reference to anything else* within it or without it, regardless of all force and all reason. Now, the world is full of this element of irresponsible, free Originality," and so on. (*Collected Papers*, vol. 2, 45–46). We must notice that in Lispector, reaching Originality comes after the failure of language, that is, the failure of mediation, which is the third of Peirce's categories (Originality is second, after Binarity). Once there is mediation, there is no absolute before/after. This must be taken into consideration to understand that the mystical is not, or it is not only, an absolute term of the regime of mediation. It is also and always a strengthening of it, as the very existence of mystical literature shows.

22. Marguerite Porete writes, "*tout ce quen l'en peut de Dieu dire ne escrire, ne que l'enpeut penser, qui plus est que n'est dire, est assez mieulx mentir que ce n'est vray dire*" ("all that can be said or written about God, or that we can think of Him, which is more than saying, is much more a lying than telling the truth"). (Marguerite Porete, *Le mirouer des simples ames*, ed. Romana Guarnieri. Corpus Christianorum Continuatio Mediaevalis LXIX (Turnhout, Belgium: Brepols Publishers, 1986), 334.

23. Carolyn G. Heilbrun, *Writing a Woman's Life* (New York: W. W. Norton, 1988), 23. The expression "rhetoric of uncertainty" comes originally from Patricia Spacks. "To start telling the truth" summarizes a passage in which the American semiologist Teresa de Lauretis reproposes the political practice of consciousness-raising (in Italy this is called *autocoscienza* by Carla Lonzi) in order to modify the relationship with given reality and to make women's experience sayable (46). Heilbrun states, "In simple words, we must start telling the truth, as a group, to one another."

Chapter 3

1. F. Braudel, "History and the Social Sciences: The *Longue Durée*," *On History*, trans. Sarah Matthews (Chicago: University of Chicago Press, 1980), 57–92. I will often quote this book because it has shed light on part of my research.

2. The famous book by Philippe Ariès, *Centuries of Childhood*, trans. Robert Baldick (New York: Alfred A. Knopf, 1962), contains the first observations in the constitution of the paradigm of the importance of childhood. In our century Freud and Melanie Klein have given a theoretical systematization to this paradigm.

3. Adrienne Rich, *Of Woman Born* (New York: W. W. Norton & Company, 1986), 11. To the problem posed by the state of need, we prefer, for instance, the response of rights (of the sick, the handicapped, etc.). In *The Grammar of Justice*, Elizabeth Wolgast discusses the weakness of that response. I have written that the practical response of imitating little girls and boys is clearly precluded in our culture. This is obvious, but why, exactly? Is it precluded by a feeling of humiliation? As is well known, the Gospel invites us to imitate "little children" ["*piccoli*"], a principle that has been followed by those in search of Christian perfection. One of the best known among these religious figures is Thérèse Martin of the religious order of the Discalced Carmelites. She is also known as "little Thérèse," to associate her with and distinguish her from the great Teresa of Avila, the founder of the order. A less well-known figure is Caterina Vannini (1562–1606), who ends her career as a young prostitute with penitence and mystical research through her correspondence with Federico Borromeo. See Giovanni Pozzi and Claudio Leonardi, eds., *Scrittrici mistiche italiane* [*Italian Mystical Women Writers*] (Genoa: Marietti, 1988), 399–418. Yet in our culture, childhood religious culture has not encouraged the capacity and the inclination of people to learn from little boys and girls. Is this perhaps because the feeling of humiliation has not been eliminated, but, instead, it has been used for ascetic purposes? However, this is not always the case. The beguine Marguerite Porete takes childhood as an example of freedom. She states that a free soul neither does anything nor gives up anything for God. In this it is like children: "*Regardez l'enfant qui est pur innocent: fait il chose ne lesse a faire pour grant ne pour petit, se il ne luy plaist?*" ["Think of the child who is genuinely innocent: does the child do or stop doing something for adults or for children if the child does not want to?"] (*Le mirouer des simples ames*, ed. Romana Guarnieri, Corpus Christianorum Continuatio Mediaevalis LXI 98). I must add, however, that the imitation of children as a solution to the condition of need is practiced more widely than we see it. In fact, both the perception and the actual behavior are equally precluded by our culture.

4. D. W. Winnicott, *Human Nature* (London: Free Association Books, 1988), 179.

5. Winnicott, op. cit., 110.

6. Parmenides quoted in E. Severino, "Ritornare a Parmenide" ["Return to Parmenides"], *Rivista di filosofia neo-scolastica*, 1964, fasc. II, 141.

7. Winnicott, op. cit., 111.

8. Ibid.

9. Ibid.

10. Winnicott, op. cit., 114. When I examined how Winnicott falls into the nihilism of the "illusion of a contact with the external reality," I pointed out how he leaps improperly from the experience of external reality in relation to the mother to that of the individual's point of view; in other words, in Winnicott's theory the solipsistic conception of the "I" takes over. In our culture, there is a great difficulty in holding fast to the subject's point of view in a constitutive relationship with an other. Such a relationship is considered alienating, and consequently, by definition, it does not constitute a point of view. On this subject, Edith Stein's *On the Problem of Empathy* (1917) is an innovative text that has not been appreciated enough. In her book Stein describes empathy as an originary lived experience not for the subject but for an other, and experienced as such by the subject. "In my non-originary experience I feel, as it were, led by an originary one not experienced by me but still there, manifesting itself in my nonoriginary experience" (*On the Problem of Empathy*, trans. Waltraut Stein [The Hague: Martinus Nijhoff, 1964], 11, translation modified).

11. "A *Third* is something which brings a First into relation to a Second. A sign is a sort of a Third. How shall we characterize it? (. . .) It appears to me that the essential function of a sign is to render inefficient relations efficient—not to set them into action, but to establish a habit or general rule whereby they will act on occasion." C. S. Peirce, *Collected Papers*, vol. 8, section 8.333, 227.

12. Julia Kristeva, *Revolution in Poetic Language*, trans. Margaret Wallace (New York: Columbia University Press, 1984), 15–45.

13. Winnicott, op. cit., 104, 137.

14. Rich, 203.

15. Luce Irigaray, "The Universal as Mediation" and "A Chance for Life," *Sexes and Genealogies*, trans. Gillian Gill (New York: Columbia University Press, 1993), respectively, 125–49 and 183–206.

16. Kristeva, 43–45.

17. Scuola di Barbiana, *Lettera a una professoressa* (Florence: Libreria editrice Fiorentina, 1967).

18. R. Jakobson, *Selected Writings*, 2: 239–59.

19. G. Bateson, "The Cybernetics of the "Self": A Theory of Alcoholism," *Steps to an Ecology of the Mind* (New York: Ballantine Books, 1972), 313. I have inevitably produced a parallelism between God and the mother. In my text the God of the alcoholics seems to correspond to the mother. However, this is not correct and could mislead. The mother's surplus is her position of initial and irreversible superiority with respect to my singularity and freedom. "What comes before a woman is her mother; there is no other name" (the Milan Women's Bookstore Collective, op. cit., 112). As I have said, women

who become mothers do not automatically become grander than others. The fact that I have a son makes me a mother, which is a title of social merit and not of human grandeur. On the contrary, the woman who brought me into the world is grand because she comes before me, because she is the fount of my every choice and grandeur. This makes her grandeur unique and unparalleled.

20. I use the word *habit* according to the meaning Peirce gives to this word. I refrain from summarizing that meaning for fear of making the concept banal. As Peirce himself suggests, it is enough to think of habit as "a sufficiently close analogue of a modification of consciousness," and it is enough to know that habit is "the real and living logical conclusion" of every process of a symbolic nature. C. S. Peirce, *Collected Papers of Charles Sanders Peirce*, ed. Charles Hartshorne and Paul Weiss, vol. 5 (Cambridge: University Press, 1934), 332 and 341.

21. F. Saussure, *Course in General Linguistics*, ed. Charles Bally and Albert Sechehaye and trans. Wade Baskin (New York: McGraw-Hill, 1966), 9.

22. Saussure, op. cit., 77–78.

23. Hans Kelsen, *General Theory of Law and State*, trans. Anders Wedberg (New York: Russell & Russell, 1961), 33. My idea of an agreement with the real through the mediation of the mother echoes the notion of an originary agreement between the subject and the world formulated by the philosopher of language Wilhelm von Humboldt. See Lia Formigari, *L'esperienza e il segno* [*Experience and Sign*] (Rome: Editori Riuniti, 1990), 233 and following pages.

Chapter 4

1. The opposition between sex and gender (which corresponds roughly to the opposition between nature and culture) is present in English-language feminist literature more often than in Continental European literature, whose position toward it is expressed well by Luce Irigaray in a note from "The Universal as Mediation": "Hegel and his translators consistently use the word *gender*, but sometimes I have substituted *sex*. In fact, the word *gender* is used to designate the difference of the sexes as well as grammatical gender. But gender in grammar expresses the reality of the two sexes in a very diverse and unequal way. If we are going to reconsider the question of culture and its systems of representation on the basis of sexualized bodies as places where different subjectivities are located, we need to take issue with the economy of grammatical gender. Hence, the necessity to separate the two notions of *gender* and *sex* in order to dialecticize a point that Hegel never differentiated. Thus, the word *sex* is used in regard to male and female persons and not just to male and female genital organs." Luce Irigaray, *Sexes and Genealogies*, trans. Gillian C. Gill (New York: Columbia University Press, 1993), 127–28. I find

it intriguing how the opposition gender/sex has always been the cause of disagreement among North American feminists. Evelyn Fox Keller, a supporter of the theoretical and political value of that opposition, states, "In America, feminism started out by making the distinction between sex and gender, which has never been truly followed." The effects of this should be critiqued, and I agree with Keller that "today the difficulty in recognizing the difference between the gender and the nature of a female sexed body—the fact of having a female body—has brought feminist theory to completely reject the whole question of sex and gender, and to speak instead in terms of 'difference' in a generic sense; that is, within other cultural, ethnic differences, all considered at the same level" (from "Conversazione con Evelyn Fox Keller" ["Discussion with Evelyn Fox Keller"], *Lapis* 9 [1990]: 3). The problem raised is caused by the lack of awareness of the symbolic and, consequently, by not taking it into consideration. This gets even worse the moment we claim to solve the problem of sex/gender difference by opposing gender and sex. I think that this opposition conveys the idea that the mother's weaving [*confezione*] of the body can be separated from its cultural meanings; in other words, that the mother does not think or that her thinking is a scarcely relevant aspect of her work.

2. The phrase "saving the phenomena" is the answer that G. Bontadini gives to E. Severino's invitation "to return to Parmenides": "Sozein tà fainómena. A Emanuele Severino" ["Saving the Phenomena: To Emanuele Severino"], *Conversazioni di metafisica* [*Conversations on Metaphysics*], 2 vols. (Milan, Italy: Vita e Pensiero, 1971), 2: 136–66. What I say about ancient philosophy is based on this text by Bontadini.

3. Sigmund Freud, *The Standard Edition of the Complete Psychological Works of Sigmund Freud*, trans. James Strachey, 24 vols. (London: The Hogarth Press, 1911–13), vol. 12, 67–68.

4. Luce Irigaray, *Thinking the Difference*, trans. Karin Montin (New York: Routledge, 1994), 111.

5. J. Lacan, *Seminar VII: The Ethics of Psychoanalysis 1959–1960*, ed. Jacques-Alain Miller and trans. Dennis Porter (New York: W. W. Norton, 1992), 53–54; *Erlebnis* is a German word that can be translated as living or lived experience.

6. The semiologist and novelist Umberto Eco summarizes Levi-Strauss's thesis of the exchange of women, articulated in *The Elementary Structures of Kinship*, trans. James Harle Bell and John Richard von Sturmer, ed. Rodney Needham (Boston: Beacon Press, 1969), as follows: "Let us now consider the exchange of women. In what sense can this be considered a symbolic process? In this context, women would appear to be *physical objects* to be used through physiological operations (to be *consumed* as in the case of food and other goods) . . . However, if the woman were merely the physical body with which the husband enters into sexual relations in order to produce sons, it could not

then be explained why *every* man does not copulate with *every* woman. Why is man obliged by certain conventions to choose one (or more, according to custom) woman, following very precise and inflexible rules of choice? Because it is only the woman's symbolic value which places her *in opposition*, within the system, to other women. The woman, the moment she becomes 'wife,' is no longer merely a physical body: she is a *sign* which connotes a system of social obligations." (U. Eco, *A Theory of Semiotics* (Bloomington: Indiana University Press, 1976), 26. This passage by Eco is a page of scientific prose worthy of Paul Julius Moebius, a weigher of brains and author of *L'inferiorita mentale della donna: una fonte del razzismo antifemminile* [*Mental Inferiority of Women: A Source of Racism toward Women*] (Torino: Einaudi, 1978).

     7. See Diotima, "La nostra comune capacità d'infinito" ["Our Common Capacity for the Infinite"], *Diotima: mettere al mondo il mondo* (Milan, Italy: La Tartaruga, 1990), 61–76.

     8. Melanie Klein, "Envy and Gratitude," in *Envy and Gratitude and Other Works 1946–1963*, ed. M. Masud R. Khan (London: Hogarth Press, 1975). This is how Melanie Klein recounts the happy resolution of one of her patients' cases: "The response to the analysis of the dream was a striking change in the emotional situation. The patient now experienced a feeling of happiness and gratitude more vividly than in previous analytic sessions. She had tears in her eyes, which was unusual, and said that she felt as if she now had had an entirely satisfactory feed. It also occurred to her that her breast-feeding and her infancy might have been happier than she had assumed. Also, she felt more hopeful about the future and the result of her analysis. The patient had more fully realized one part of herself, which was by no means unknown to her in other connections. She was aware that she was envious and jealous of various people but had not been able to recognize it sufficiently in the relation to the analyst because it was too painful to experience that she was envying and spoiling the analyst as well as the success of the analysis. In this session, after the interpretations referred to, her envy had lessened; the capacity for enjoyment and gratitude had come to the fore, and she was able to experience the analytic session as a happy feed" (205–6).

     9. Lucy Freeman, *The Story of Anna O* (New York: Walker and Company, 1972). Anna O's case, presented by Joseph Breuer, is recounted by Breuer and Sigmund Freud in *Studies on Hysteria* in S. Freud, *Standard Edition*, vol. 2, 21–47.

     10. "The political practice of consciousness-raising was invented in the U.S., we do not know by whom, toward the end of the 60's." The Milan Women's Bookstore Collective, *Sexual Difference*, trans. Patricia Cicogna and Teresa de Lauretis (Bloomington: Indiana University Press, 1990), 40. I wonder if the therapy of recovery of Alcoholics Anonymous was a precedent for the practice of *autocoscienza*. "To be precise, American women were talking about

'consciousness-raising.' In Italy it was called *autocoscienza* [*self-consciousness*], a term adopted by Carla Lonzi, who organized one of the first Italian groups to adopt that practice. Groups of women met to talk about themselves, or about anything else, as long as it was based on their own personal experience. These groups were intentionally kept small and were no part of larger organizations" (ibid, 40, trans. modified). Carla Lonzi (1931–82) is the founder of the group Rivolta femminile and of a publishing house called Scritti di rivolta femminile, which published her political writings such as *Sputiamo su Hegel* [*Let's Spit on Hegel*] (1970), *La donna clitoridea e la donna vaginale* [*Clitoral Woman and Vaginal Woman*] (1970), *Taci, anzi parla* [*Shut Up, or Rather Speak Up*] (1978).

11. Jane Austen, *Persuasion* (London: Penguin Books, 1965), 248. In emphasizing the surprising grandeur of Jane Austen, I must also note that I do not believe the "myth" of the provincial isolation in which Jane Austen supposedly lived. Malcom Skey, editor of Austen's minor works, states, "However, the old myth according to which Austen knew nothing at all of the outside world must be discredited, even if in her novels she rarely refers to it." Jane Austen, *Sanditon*, trans. Linda Gaia, ed. Malcom Skey (Rome-Naples: Edizioni Theoria, 1990), 15.

12. Lispector, op. cit., 173.

13. I will explain the second trichotomy of Peirce's semiotics by giving some quotes from Peirce. "Anything (. . .) is an Icon of anything, in so far as it is like that thing and used as a sign (. . .). An *Index* is a sign which refers to the Object that it denotes by virtue of being really affected by that Object (. . .). A *Symbol* is a sign which refers to the Object that it denotes by virtue of a law, usually an association of general ideas, which operates to cause the Symbol to be interpreted as referring to that Object" (C. S. Peirce, *Collected Papers of Charles Sanders Peirce*, ed. Charles Hartshorne and Paul Weiss, vol. 2 [Cambridge: Harvard University Press, 1932], 143).

14. C. S. Peirce, *Collected Papers*, vol. 2, 166. Peirce often gives the name of law to symbolic authority. I prefer to differentiate them in order to safeguard the prospect of going beyond the law without consequently finding ourselves in chaos. In "The Epistle of Paul the Apostle to the Romans," Paul introduces into our culture the theme of going beyond the law. In his latest book, Elvio Fachinelli quotes this letter in order to correct Lacan's interpretation of it. Fachinelli writes that "he [Lacan] omits the fact that what Paul talks about is the *old* relationship with the law and that the apostle declares himself released from this law, 'he is dead to it,' in order to submit himself to the news of the Spirit instead of the *vetustas litterae*. By analyzing only the first part of Paul's discourse, Lacan limits himself to mastering the letter, the old letter, and he overlooks the fact that the new formulation, which is certainly not a substitution or a re-assumption of the old law, expresses Paul's, and together with him the whole culture's, shift. Lacan's omission is a symptom of his inability to

go beyond the order of obedience and transgression" (E. Fachinelli, *La mente estatica*) [*The Ecstatic Mind*] (Milan, Italy: Adelphi, 1989), 194.

15. I have heard Lia Cigarini of the Milan Women's Bookstore assert that the hysterical body is the major impediment to the elimination of female difference and the male appropriation of maternal power. She passed on to me the thought of the French group *Politique et Psychanalyse*, founded by Antoinette Fouque at the end of the 1960s. Part of the theoretical thought of the women's movement is transmitted orally, and this is often the newest, most disruptive part. The current system of reference to written sources does not help us to realize this and to recognize our debts to people whose thought is sometimes of primary importance; as, for instance, my intellectual debt to Lia Cigarini.

Chapter 5

1. E. Mach, *The Analysis of Sensations and the Relation of the Physical to the Psychical*, trans. C. M. Williams and Sydney Waterlow (New York: Dover, 1959), 333. We can find a similar opinion and more thorough point of view in C. S. Peirce, "Pragmatism and Abduction," in *Collected Papers of Charles Sanders Peirce*, vol. 5.

2. See above, chapter 2, note 11.

3. In a manuscript I hope to see published soon.

4. My feminist friend referred to Luce Irigaray, *Speculum of the Other Woman* (Ithaca, NY: Cornell University Press, 1985), trans. Gillian C. Gill.

5. The thesis according to which the difference between being a man or a woman is only due to the cultural codes in power is also maintained in the United States by a number of so-called poststructuralist feminists, although with some contradictions as the following short example shows. The catalog of a publishing house that seems to be in the vanguard of poststructuralism presents its feminist books in the perspective of "differences of class, race, cultural tradition, nationality, religious beliefs, sexual preferences and definitions of gender" (Cornell University Press, *New and Recent Books in Women's Studies*, s.d., p. 2). In this catalog only sexual difference has been reduced to its definition, so why not also give definitions of the other differences of race, and so on? According to the poststructuralist way of thinking, differences of class, race, and so forth are also subject to the way cultural codes represent them. However, the catalog admits implicitly that the representation of those differences, no matter how prescribed they are by cultural codes, re-presents to us, while interpreting it, something that is already present in our experience, whereas only sexual difference disappears and is replaced by its definitions, which then become the only things we can talk about. The difficulty arises

from the fact that a thought of sexual difference and a politics of it perhaps could not exist without being aware of the determining power that cultural codes have over what we think we are and what we actually are. In fact, this awareness has made it possible for us no longer to identify ourselves with male representations of being woman, without for that reason having to reject the fact that we are women. Evelyn Fox Keller writes, "feminism started out by making the distinction between sex and gender" (see above, chapter 4, note 1). This distinction, however, does not lead anywhere in the static critical way of thinking. We need to reconsider the sex/gender distinction in terms of the complete circle of mediation, in which the body is on the merry-go-round [*il girotondo*], if I can call it so, with the word, and the interpreted becomes the interpreter and the interpreter the interpreted.

      6. See W. W. Bartley III, *L. Wittgenstein e K. R. Popper maestri di scuola elementare* [*L. Wittgenstein and K. R. Popper: Teachers of Elementary School*], trans. D. Antiseri (Rome: Armando, 1976).

      7. Hegel, *Phenomenology of Spirit*, op. cit., 288.

      8. I have already told this story ("Il pensatore neutro era una donna" ["The neuter thinker was a woman"], in *Inchiesta*, anno XVII, n. 77, July–September 1987, 21–23). This story has been a turning point in my life, not because of the event in itself, that actually could have killed me, but because it happened, not accidentally, between the publication of the special issue of *Sottosopra* [*Upside Down*] titled "Piu donne che uomini" ["More Women than Men"], January 1983, and the constitution of *Fontana del ferro*, the group that later founded Diotima, thanks to which I became a philosopher.

      9. There is a criterion for distinguishing the contextually true from the relatively true. Unlike the relatively true, the contextually true can be translated into other contexts. I developed R. Jakobson's notion of a "translatability in context" in my *Maglia e uncinetto* [*Knitting and Crochet*] (Milan, Italy: Feltrinelli, 1981), 84 and following pages. Einstein's special and general theory of relativity explains how the contextually true is given as something that can be translated from one context to another. In mathematical physics, this translation can easily be done with a few mathematical equations, whereas in human reality things are more complex and compelling. (Author's note: At school, when I happen to talk about Einstein I begin by saying: there is an abyss between relativity and relativism. Then I conclude by saying: as you can see, relativity has triumphed over relativism.)

      10. K. Marx, *Grundrisse: Foundations of the Critique of Political Economy (Rough Draft)*, trans Martin Nicolaus (New York: Penguin, 1973), 162–63. Marx begins his analysis with the transformation of commodities into exchange value. "But the transformation of the commodity into exchange value does not equate it to any other particular commodity, but expresses it as equivalent, expresses its exchangeability relation, *vis-à-vis* all other commodities" (144). Then Marx

introduces the symbol of exchangeability: "such a symbol presupposes general recognition; it can only be a social symbol; it expresses, indeed, nothing more than a social relation" (ibid.). Here Marx inserts the decisive factor: "Because the product becomes a commodity, and the commodity becomes an exchange value, it obtains, at first only in the head, a double existence . . . as a natural product on one side, as exchange value on the other" (145). At this point money appears: "The exchange value which is separated from commodities and exists alongside them as itself a commodity, this is—*money*" (ibid.).

11. Marx, op. cit., 163.

12. Marx, op. cit., 157.

13. Marx, op. cit., 160. A few pages earlier Marx writes, "The dissolution of all products and activities into exchange values presupposes the dissolution of all fixed personal (historic) relations of dependence in production, as well as the all-sided dependence of the producers on one another . . . This reciprocal dependence is expressed in the constant necessity for exchange, and in exchange value as the all-sided mediation" (Marx, op. cit., 156). In this text Marx explains the symbolic power of the market, which also seems to be the presupposition for the discovery of the symbolic on the part of the philosophers of our century. Unlike Marx, Saussure considers acceptable the comparison between money and language: "To determine what a five-franc piece is worth one must therefore know: (1) that it can be exchanged for a fixed quantity of a different thing, e.g. bread; and (2) that it can be compared with a similar value of the same system, e.g. a one-franc piece, or with coins of another system (a dollar, etc.). In the way a word can be exchanged for something dissimilar, an idea; besides, it can be compared with something of the same nature, another word." Saussure makes an analogous distinction to what Marx says about use value and exchange value to demonstrate that "[a word] is endowed not only with a signification but also and especially with a value, and this is something quite different." F. Saussure, *Course in General Linguistics*, trans. Wade Baskin (New York: McGraw-Hill Book Company, 1966), 115.

14. On this theme I consider of fundamental importance A. Sohn-Rethel, *Intellectual and Manual Labour: A Critique of Epistemology* (Atlantic Highlands, NJ: Humanities Press, 1978). The question I am raising has been expressed in the same way by Sohn-Rethel in "Denaro e filosofia. Incontro con Alfred SohnRethel" ["Money and Philosophy: A Meeting with Alfred Sohn-Rethel"], trans. F. Coppellotti, ed. Helmut Hoge, *Linea d'Ombra* [*Line of Shadow*], 51 (1990), 60–64.

15. Marx, op. cit., 162. Arguing over liberation from the domination of the capitalist mode of production, the philosopher and economist Claudio Napoleoni sees in women an element of resistance to such domination. "In fact, there are residues, parts of realities, that escape from this mode of pro-

duction. . . . Among all the possible residues the most important is probably women. Women stand outside this mode of production as a consequence of their systematic condition and not only as women's individual situation. Precisely because of the systematic condition of being woman, of being human in a female condition, women are outside this relation of production, which is like a circle of production controlling quantity, a circle in which quality is systematically reduced. It is for this reason that throughout all of history up to today—but mainly in a specific way in the history of the bourgeois capitalist world—women are marginalized and oppressed. That is why women are outside the relation of production, and this is in all probability an important and pervasive residue." "La liberazione dal dominio e la tradizione marxista" ["Liberation from Domination and the Marxist Tradition"] (1986) in C. Napoleoni, *Cercate ancora. Lettera sulla laicita e ultimi scritti* [*Keep on Searching: A Letter on Laicality and Last Writings*], ed. Raniero La Valle (Rome: Editori Riuniti, 1990), 46. This seems to me a remarkable approximation of the thought of sexual difference and the theme of female estrangement. Both Napoleoni's and Marx's theory lack the idea of symbolic order. Consequently, they risk basing women's resistance on their procreative function, thereby denying the principle of women's freedom.

Chapter 6

1. When I say, "*as a consequence* of the new combination," I am referring to a logical sequence rather than a temporal sequence. The process I am describing here, that is, the leap from a vicious circle to a "virtuous" circle, takes place temporally, but once this process is finished it is not temporal anymore. This might seem nonsense: isn't our lived experience immersed in temporality? If we accept the fact that time is a mediator for the thinkability of our experience, instead of its theater, we must admit that there could be processes which, once they reach their logical conclusion, "escape" time. Besides the example given in the text, another instance is the statement "now we have always been free," which concluded Diotima's discussion on women's freedom. However, the paradoxical form of statements like this tells us that we are not beyond the necessity of mediation.

2. Evelyn Fox Keller, *Reflections on Gender and Science* (New Haven, CT: Yale University Press, 1985), 110.

3. Keller, op. cit., 114.

4. Keller, op. cit., 107.

5. Keller, op. cit., 110.

6. The text of that meeting was recorded and published in *Associazione donne insegnanti di Firenze* [*Association of Women Teachers of Florence*],

"Inviolabilità del corpo femminile" ["The Inviolability of the Female Body"], Atti del Corso di aggiornamento [Records of the Refresher Course], Florence (March 2–May 11, 1990), 15–32.

    7. The sayable and the desirable do not need mediation to the same extent. The mediation needed by the sayable is great, whereas that of desire is very little, perhaps none. I am referring to the existence of a desire, not to our awareness of its existence, and even less to the way desire is formulated and satisfied. These are stages that require a crescendo of mediations. In fact, the existence of an unknown desire can signal itself in indirect ways that psychoanalysis teaches us how to decipher. The awareness of the necessity of mediation to accompany our own desires makes it easier and more effective to satisfy them. Listening to our desires is a way to oppose the domination of inadequate cultural codes because it forces us to find new forms of mediation. Simone Weil writes, "The only thing in us that is unconditioned is desire" (Simone Weil, *First and Last Notebooks*, op. cit., 143).

    8. F. Braudel, "History and Social Sciences: The *Longue Durée*," *On History*, trans. Sarah Matthews (Chicago: University of Chicago Press, 1980), 39 (see above, chapter 3, note 1).

    9. Braudel, op. cit., 39.

    10. On this point I disagree with Adriana Cavarero, friend and fellow researcher in philosophy. After having persuasively proposed "focusing on the category of birth," Adriana Cavarero writes, "Therefore a significant result of the philosophical shift in perspective on birth is a narrowing of the societal sphere. This sets limits on both legislation and the political symbolic order, which must divest itself of its totalizing and evangelizing aims, allowing the meaning of human life to exist outside the confines of the polis." Adriana Cavarero, *In Spite of Plato: A Feminist Rewriting of Ancient Philosophy* (New York: Routledge, 1995), 83–84. I think that, on the one hand, Cavarero's critique does not fit with the modern notion and practice of politics, and that, on the other hand, it conforms too much to the idea of separating the public from the private sphere—an idea that the politics of women has put into question.

    11. Luisa Muraro, *Guglielma e Maifreda. Storia di una eresia femminile* [*Guglielma and Maifreda: Story of a Female Heresy*] (Milan, Italy: La Tartaruga, 1985).

    12. Evelyn Fox Keller, interview, "Interrogando amorosamente la scienza. Conversazione con Evelyn Fox Keller" ["Lovingly Interrogating Science: Discussion with Evelyn Fox Keller"] by Paola Melchiori and Luciana Percovich, *Lapis* (September 1990).

    13. Elisabetta Rasy, *La lingua delta nutrice* [*The Language of the Wet-Nurse*] (Rome: Edizioni delle donne, 1978), 115. Besides the passage I already quoted, there are some others to support my idea: "Women are marginalized, isolated

from the 'center.' From its supposed externality, feminism rediscovers itself as a movement 'inside' other movements or institutionalized situations of the social (. . .). This idea of internality in relation to the social and the political marks the passage from the feminist movement to the women's movement" (Rasy 17); "Feminism (. . .) reproduces and displays the forbidden relationship of women with the social, with the symbolic order" (Rasy 19); "for fear of recognizing in the female women's estrangement within society, united and organized women are considered the last available 'elsewhere' ['*altrove*']. A utopia (. . .) or a land to conquer: all Italian political parties are trying a new way to colonize. The new colonization is no longer based on an implied contempt, but, rather, on a proclaimed esteem for women. From 'invisible,' women become 'better'" (Rasy 19).

14. Bibi Tomasi, *La sproporzione* [*The Disproportion*] (Milan, Italy: La Tartaruga, 1980).

15. On this point I agree again with Adriana Cavarero. In her comment on a document by women on the decriminalization of abortion, Cavarero writes that our "most realistic weapon" lies in "frontally opposing to the invasiveness of the law the maternal power with respect to generation, as a place that *per se* resists any regulation" (*In Spite of Plato*, 79, translation modified).

16. In the course of the persecution of witches, some kind of meaningful interaction was ultimately established both by the men in power (as, for instance, the classic R. Mandrou, *Magistrats et sorciers en France au XVII siècle* [*Magistrates and Witches in Seventeenth Century France*] [Paris: Pion, 1968], shows) and by the victims, although this is harder to point out. However, this interaction was a process as slow and partial, as long and chaotic as the persecution of witches was. We must always remember that the persecution of witches has accompanied the formation of modern society step by step, whereas the tendency would be to relegate it to medieval history. One of the very first episodes of this persecution concludes in Milan in 1390. The two victims were Sibilla and Pierina, two women who worshiped a female divinity they called Madonna Oriente and Signora del gioco. See my *La signora del gioco* [*The Lady of the Game*] (Milan, Italy: Feltrinelli, 1976), 147–55. I would like to conclude my present work with the memory of these two women and their mysterious religion.

Index

affirmation, xxvi, xxviii, xxx, 20–23, 31, 43, 58, 103n8
Agamben, Giorgio, xxviii
Alcoholics Anonymous, 45, 112–13n10
Anna O. (Bertha Pappenheim), 59, 112n9
Ariès, Phillipe, 123n2
Aristotle, xxvi, 25–26, 53, 87, 103n9, 105n12
art, 9, 18, 36, 41–43, 49, 73, 90, 103n8
Association of Women Teachers of Florence, 117n6
attachment, 10–11, 13, 56–59, 61, 66–67, 70, 76, 97, 100n13
Austen, Jane, xii, xxvi, 61–62, 113n11
authority, viii–ix, xi–xv, xxvi, xxviii, xxx, 6–8, 18, 31–32, 46–47, 57, 62, 65, 67, 69, 72–73, 87, 95–97, 106n13, 113n14. *See also* power
autonomy, ix, xxvii, 48, 86–88, 93–94

Baeri, Emma, 70
Bartley III, W. W., 115n6
Bateson, Gregory, 45, 81, 106n13, 109n19
becoming, 31, 34, 47, 53, 72, 88, 104n11

being, xii, xxvii, xxix, 4, 6–7, 18, 21–31, 33–34, 36–40, 42–43, 45, 48, 53, 55–56, 59, 65, 67, 69–70, 76, 81–82, 85, 87, 94, 98, 101n2, 103n8, 104n11, 106n18, 107n21, 114n5, 117n15
Bergson, Henri, 34
birth, 7, 18–19, 36, 40, 75, 96, 101n1, 118n10
blockage, vii, xxvi–xxvii, 3, 30–31, 39, 44–46, 49
body, viii, ix–xiv, xxvii–xxviii, 12–13, 21, 37, 41, 45, 48, 57–58, 66, 75, 77, 81, 91, 95, 97–98, 101n2, 110–11n1, 111n6, 114n15, 115n5, 118n6
Boema, Guglielma, xxix, 91–92, 118n11
Bontadini, Gustavo, xxiv, 25–27, 103n8, 104n11, 105n12, 106n17, 111n2
Borromeo, Federico, 108n3
Bosotti, Piera, xxxiii
Braudel, Fernand, xxvi, 35, 89–90, 107n1, 118n8–9
Breuer, Joseph 59, 112n9
Bukharin, Nikolai, 104n11

capitalism, xxix, xxxn11, 70, 116n15
Capra, Fritjof, 106n13

Cavarero, Adriana, xxiv, xxvi, xxx, 118n10, 119n15
Centro documentazione donna di Firenze, 67
child, childhood, viii–xv, xxiii, xxvi–xxviii, 4, 12, 19, 23, 35–45, 48–49, 51–52, 65, 69, 73, 76, 80–81, 85, 95, 97, 101n1, 108n2–3. *See also* fetus; infant; newborn
Chodorow, Nancy, xvn4
Cigarini, Lia, xxiv, 114n15
code, 48–49, 64, 75, 78, 89, 96, 103n8, 114n5, 118n7
commodity, 58, 78–80, 115–16n10
Compton-Burnett, Ivy, 33
consciousness, 19, 45, 50, 70, 72, 90, 104n9, 107n21, 110n20
consciousness raising [*autocoscienza*], xii, xxv, 20, 59, 70, 75, 107n23, 112n10
Copernicus, Nicolaus, 103n8
correspondence, ix, xiv, 1–2, 24–26, 36, 40, 43, 55, 74, 78, 85, 90
Cosentino, Vita, 50
creating couple (mother/child), 37–40, 52, 64–65
critique, xii, xxvi, 12–13, 20–23, 25, 34, 80, 82, 101n2–3, 111n1, 118n10
culture, vii, ix, xxv, 3–4, 7, 9–10, 14, 17–19, 21–23, 26–27, 31–33, 35–36, 39–40, 42, 48, 51–52, 56, 58, 62, 66–67, 71–72, 74–76, 88, 92–93, 97, 103n8, 108n3, 109n10, 110–11n1, 113n14, 114–15n5, 118n7

Dante Alighieri, 98
daughter, xii–xiii, xxvii, 10, 13–14, 23, 40, 42, 52, 55, 66, 87, 102n7
D.B., (friend) 40, 42
Derrida, Jacques, 12

Descartes, x, xxvi, 3–4, 9, 27–29, 99n3, 99n5, 99n7, 101n2, 106n16
desire, 3–4, 9, 15, 17, 22–24, 33, 37, 56, 95, 99n13, 101n1, 118n7
Diotima, xv, xxiv–xxvi, xxx, xxxiii, 50, 112n7, 115n8, 117n1
disparity, viii, xxviii, 46–47, 49

Eckhart, Meister, 105–6n13
Eco, Umberto, 111–12n6
economics, xxvi, 70, 80, 89, 115n10, 116n15
education, 8, 14, 46, 62. *See also* school
Einstein, Albert, 25, 104n10, 115n9
empiricism, 26, 72, 105n12
entrustment, viii, xi, xxv, 19, 45, 49
epistemology, 25, 45, 92, 104n10, 106n15
equality, viii, xii–xiii, xxv, xxviii, xxx, 14, 102n3
ethics, 73–74, 82, 88
Euripedes, 7
experience, viii–xii, xv, xxv, xxvii, 1, 3–4, 7–8, 13, 20, 25–26, 30–39, 43, 50, 52–53, 55–58, 61, 63–64, 66, 69–79, 88–89, 91–95, 97, 101n1, 106n13, 107n23, 109n10, 111n5, 112n8, 113n10, 114n5, 117n1

Fachinelli, Elvio, xxiv, 81, 106n13, 113–14n14
falsehood, 2, 4, 8, 10, 24, 27–29, 31, 37, 43, 76, 81, 103n8
father, viii, xi, xiii–xv, xxiii, 3, 11–14, 20, 26, 39–40, 42, 51, 58, 67, 87, 99–100n13, 101n1
F.C., (friend) 45
female, xi, xv, xxiv–xxviii, xxx, 12, 14–15, 20, 23, 27, 31–33, 46,

49–50, 52, 56–59, 61–62, 66–67, 70, 75–76, 82, 91–94, 97–98, 99–100n13, 110–11n1, 114n15, 117n15, 119n13, 119n16
feminine, 15, 30, 48, 50, 67, 102
feminism, vii, xviii, xxiii–xxx, 12, 15, 17–18, 20, 23, 52, 70, 73, 86, 101n1, 101–2n3, 110–11n1, 114–15n4–5, 118n10, 119n13
fetus, 40, 57. *See also* child; infant; newborn
fixation, xxvii, 53–58, 66, 82
flesh, 4, 18, 42, 59, 70, 75, 77, 81, 101n1, 105n12
Fliess, Wilhelm, 103n9
Formigari, Lia, 101n2, 110n23
Foucault, Michel, 12
foundation, viii, xxvi, 2–4, 9, 11, 19, 101n2, 105n12
Fouque, Antoinette, 114n15
Frederick II, (emperor) 48
freedom, xxvii, 5–6, 10, 13, 15, 21, 31, 33, 45, 47, 49, 68, 70, 72, 76, 83, 87, 89, 94–95, 98, 100n13, 102n3, 107n21, 108n3, 109n19, 116n15, 117n15, 117n1
Freeman, Lucy, 112n9
Freud, Sigmund, viii, xxvi, 7, 10, 13–14, 24, 33–34, 42, 48, 53–54, 57, 59, 67, 99–100n13, 103n9, 108n2, 111n3, 112n9

gender, xii, xiv, xxvii, 52, 75, 102n3, 110–11n1, 114–15n5. *See also* sex
genealogy, xxiv, 42, 66
generation, 4, 6–8, 19, 23, 25, 78, 119n15
gift, 8–10, 44–45, 71
Gramsci, Antonio, xxviii, 70, 104–105n11
gratitude, 29, 88, 112n8
Graziani, Francesca, 50

Guarnieri, Romana, 107n22, 108n3
Guglielma. *See* Boema, Guglielma

habit, 4, 45, 109n11, 110n20
Hadewijch of Antwerp, 105n13
Hegel, Georg Wilhelm Friedrich, vii, xxvi–xxvii, xxx, 2, 22, 36, 76, 99n1–2, 110n4, 113n10, 115n7
Heidegger, Martin, xiv, xxvi, 34, 103n8
Heilbrun, Carolyn G., xxvi, 31, 107n23
Heresy, xxv, 91–92, 118n11
Hirsch, Marianne, 102n3
history, 3, 7, 9–11, 14, 24, 26–28, 30–31, 35–36, 42–43, 48–50, 70–72, 78, 89–91, 93–98, 101n2, 103n8, 104–5n11, 105n12, 106n13, 107n1, 116n13, 117n15, 119n16
Hoge, Helmut, 116n14
Humboldt, Wilhelm von, 110n23
Husserl, Edmund, x, xxvi, 3, 5, 7, 99n4, 99n8, 99n9
hysteria, xii, xxvii, 54, 56–59, 66–67, 72, 77, 112n9, 114n15

idealism, xxvii, 9, 26, 75, 101n2, 105n12
infant, xiv, 38, 54. *See also* child; fetus; newborn
injustice, xii, 7, 36, 44, 49, 103n8
Irigaray, Luce, vii, xxiv, xxvi, xxviii, xxix, 7, 12, 19, 42, 50, 55, 73, 99–100n13, 101n1, 105n12, 109n15, 110n1, 111n4, 114n4

Jakobson, Roman, xxvi, 33, 44, 47–48, 50, 109n18, 115n9

Kant, Immanuel, xii, xxvi–xxvii, 21–22, 102n4–5

Keller, Evelyn Fox, xv, xxvi, 86–87, 92–93, 96, 98, 102n3, 111n1, 115n5, 117n 2–5, 118n12

Kelsen, Hans, 26, 46, 106n15, 110n23

Klein, Melanie, xxvi, 36, 41, 59, 108n2, 112n8

Kristeva, Julia, vii–ix, xi, xiv, xv, xxvi, 40–43, 109n12, 109n16

labor, xii, xiv, 20, 22, 24, 70, 97

Lacan, Jacques, vii–viii, xxvi, 42, 48–49, 56–57, 102n4, 111n5, 113n14

language, viii–xiii, xvii, xxiv, xxvi–xxviii, xxxii, 1, 3, 6–7, 9, 13–15, 18–19, 24, 26, 29–34, 40–48, 50, 55, 59, 62–65, 67, 72–82, 88, 92–93, 95, 97, 101n2, 104n11, 107n21, 110n23, 116n13. *See also* linguistics; sayable; word

Lauretis, Teresa de, xxix, 49, 82, 102n3, 107n23, 112n10

law, viii, xxv, xxvii, 7, 9, 13, 26, 50, 64–68, 74–75, 77, 82, 89, 113n13–14, 119n15

Lazzerini, Gabriella, 50

Leonardi, Claudio, 106n13, 108n3

Lévi-Strauss, Claude, 89, 111n6

linguistics, xiii, xxiv, 5, 22, 32, 46–47, 62, 64–65, 73, 78, 80, 88, 93, 116n13. *See also* language

Lispector, Clarice, xxvi, 28–30, 63, 106n13, 106n19–21, 113n12

Little Hans, 58

Locke, John, 3

logic, xxvii, xxx, 1–2, 5, 8, 11, 14–15, 17, 20, 22–26, 33–35, 40–41, 43, 46–48, 53, 60–61, 63, 70–71, 73, 76, 83, 88, 91, 93, 95–96, 100n13, 103n8, 110n20, 117n1

Lonzi, Carla, xxv, xxx, 81–82, 107n23, 113n10

Lorenz, Konrad, 53, 70

Mach, Ernst, 25, 70, 104n10, 114n1

Maifreda da Pirovano, xxix, 91–92, 118n11

male, x, xxv, xxviii, xxx, 12, 14, 17, 20–21, 26, 33, 42, 46, 51–53, 55–56, 58, 62, 66–67, 98, 99n13, 101n1, 106n15, 110n1, 112n6, 114n15, 115n5

Mandrou, Robert, 119n16

Manzoni, Alessandro, 61, 101n2

market, 49, 70, 78–80, 96, 116n13

Martin, Thérèse, 108n3

Marx, Karl, xii, xxvi, 79–81, 89, 115–16n10–13, 116–17n15

masculine, 30, 50, 74, 101n1, 102n3

materialism, xxviii, 80, 101n2, 105n12

maternal continuum, xxvii, 52, 59, 66, 80. *See also* mother

matricide, ix, 7, 12

mediation, x, xiii, xxvii, 22, 30–32, 34, 41, 55–56, 60–64, 66–68, 70, 72–75, 77, 79, 82, 86, 88–89, 91–98, 107n21, 110n23, 115n5, 116n13, 117n1, 118n7

Melchiori, Paola, 118n12

Menenius Agrippa, 81

metaphor, viii, xv, xxvii, 2–3, 7, 18–20, 33, 41, 49–50, 65–66, 101n1

metaphysics, viii, xii, xxv–xxvi, xxviii, xxx, 21, 24–25, 36, 40, 43, 67, 69–70, 72, 75, 96, 103n8–9, 104n10–11, 105n12, 111n2

metonymy, 33, 50, 104n9

Michelet, Jules, 67

Milan Women's Bookstore, xi–xii, xviii, xxiv, xxvi, xxix, xxxiii, 49, 82, 109n19, 112n10, 114n15

mind, 2–4, 22–25, 28, 37–38, 45, 53, 60, 71–72, 74, 76, 78
Moebius, Paul Julius 112n 6
money, xxvii, 51, 78–81, 97, 116n10, 116n13, 116n14
mother: and child, viii–x, xii–xv, xxvi–xxviii, 12, 19, 23, 37–38, 40–45, 48–49, 51–52, 65, 69, 80–81, 95, 97 (*see also* creating couple); and father, viii, xi, xiii–xv, 11–14, 26, 39–40, 51, 58, 67, 87, 99–100n13, 101n1; authority of, viii–ix, xi–xiv, xxvi, 6–8, 32, 47, 62, 65, 67, 69, 72, 87, 95–97; aversion, hatred or hostility toward, x–xii, xv, 6, 10–11, 13, 21, 49, 56–58, 62, 88, 94, 100n13, 102n7; body of, xii–xiii, 37, 41, 111–12n6; childbirth, 36, 40, 96, 101n1, 118n10; knowing how to love, xxvii, 10–12, 14, 17, 19–20, 22–24, 49, 60, 66, 70, 97, 104n9, 104n11; might of, 65–66; negotiation with, viii, xii, xxvii, 11, 43–47, 49, 60; one in her place, xiii, 40, 42, 47, 50–51, 59, 82 (*see also* substitution); symbolic order of, vii, xiii, xxvii, xxxiii, 49, 62, 68, 74, 87; teaching of, viii, xii–xiii, 9–10, 19, 50, 64, 96, 101n2; tongue, 50, 59, 73–74, 77, 79, 81–82, 96, 101n2. *See also* maternal continuum
mysticism, xxv–xxvi, 25, 30, 39, 68, 81, 105–6n13, 106–7n21, 108n3

Napoleoni, Claudio, 116–17n15
nature, xii–xiii, xv, 7–9, 10, 18, 39, 51–52, 57, 66, 71, 74, 77, 110–11n1, 115–16n10
necessity, ix, xxvii, 3, 10, 12, 18, 24, 30–32, 34, 39–41, 44, 47, 56, 60–61, 63, 66, 68–74, 76–77, 82–83, 87–89, 91, 93–96, 98, 100n13, 110n1, 116n13, 117n1, 118n7
need, xii, 3, 6, 23, 28, 36–37, 45, 49–50, 65, 69, 94–95, 104n11, 108n3
negation, xxvi, 21–23, 25–26, 34, 106n18
negotiation, viii, xii, xxvii, 11, 43–47, 49, 60
Negri, Antonio, xx, xxviii–xxx
newborn, 42, 48. *See also* child; fetus; infant
nihilism, xii, xxvii, 27–32, 38, 76, 109n10

object, xi, 3, 7, 13, 22, 26, 34, 41, 43–45, 47–48, 57, 72, 79–80, 89, 97, 100n13, 104n11, 111n6, 113n13
Oedipus, 7, 42, 100n13, 101n1
origin, xiii–xiv, xxv–xxvi, xxx, 7, 9–10, 12, 14, 22–23, 25–27, 33, 38–40, 43–46, 49–56, 58–59, 63–64, 69, 73, 75, 80, 91, 93–96, 99–100n13, 104n11, 107n21, 109n10, 110n23

patriarchy, vii, x–xiv, xxv–xxix, 7, 9–11, 15, 18, 20, 23, 26–27, 31, 42, 49, 58, 88, 102n3
Paul (the apostle), 113n14
Parmenides, 3, 26, 37–38, 53, 105n12, 108n6, 111n2
Peirce, Charles Sanders, xxvi, 64, 103n8, 107n21, 109n11, 110n20, 113n13–14, 114n1
Percovich, Luciana, 118n12
philosophy, vii–viii, x–xii, xxiv–xxviii, xxxiii, 2–14, 17–18, 20–24, 26–28, 33–34, 36–38, 45, 49–50, 52–53,

philosophy *(continued)*
    55–56, 69, 71, 73, 81–82, 94, 96, 101n2, 102n3, 104n9, 104–5n11, 105n12, 106n13, 110n23, 111n2, 115n8, 116n13, 118n10
physics, 25–26, 103n9, 104n10, 115n9
Pierina di Zambello de Bugatis, 119n16
Plato, x, xii, xxiv, xxvi–xxvii, xxx, 3–8, 17, 25, 41, 53, 67, 87, 99n5–6, 99n10, 105n12, 118n10, 119n15
politics, xi–xii, xviii, xxv, xxviii–xxx, xxxiii, 6–8, 11, 33, 59, 66, 70, 72, 76, 82, 89–94, 96–97, 102n3, 107n23, 111n1, 112–13n10, 115n5, 118n10, 119n13
Politique et psychanalyse, 114n15
Pol Pot, 49
Porete, Marguerite, xxvi, xxix–xxx, 105n13, 107n22, 108n3
power, xi, xiii, xv, xxvi–xxviii, xxx, 3, 6–7, 9, 11–13, 15, 20–23, 26–27, 29, 42–43, 45, 49, 53, 58, 61, 66, 70, 73–76, 79–80, 82–83, 86–93, 96–98, 101n1, 105n12, 114n15, 114–15n5, 116n13, 119n15–16. *See also* authority
Pozzi, Giovanni, 106n13, 108n3
psychoanalysis, vii–ix, xi, xiv, xxvi, 14, 36, 42, 57, 59, 99n13, 102n4, 103n9, 111n5, 118n7
Pythagoras, 71

Rasy, Elisabetta, 48–49, 94, 118–19n13
Re, Lucia, xiv, xv, xxx
repression, 26–27, 32, 54, 67, 74, 76
Rich, Adrienne, vii, xxvi, 19, 23, 36, 42, 101n1, 102n6, 102–3n7, 108n3, 109n14
Righi, Andrea, xxx

Rovatti, Pier Aldo, xxviii
rule, 7–8, 24, 26, 33, 50, 60–61, 63–65, 68, 72–74, 76–77, 82–83, 92–94, 109n11, 112n6
Russell, Bertrand, 14

Sade, Marquis de, 13–14
sayable, xxvii, 14, 24, 28, 30–31, 43, 47, 60–61, 63–64, 74, 77–78, 93, 95, 104n11, 107n23, 118n7
Saussure, Ferdinand de, xxvi, 5, 22, 46, 93, 110n21–22, 116n13
Schopenhauer, Arthur, 22
school, 2, 17, 55, 63, 69, 73, 96, 104n9. *See also* education
science, 4, 7, 14–15, 21, 26, 37, 92, 104n10–11
Scott, Joan W., 101–2n3
Scuola di Barbiana, 109n17
semiotic, xiv, xxvi, 40–43, 113
sense of being, xii, 24–30, 34, 36–37, 39, 55, 70–71, 75–76, 82, 103n8, 106n18
Severino, Emanuele, 26–27, 103n8, 106n14, 106n18, 108n6, 111n2
sex, xxv, 7, 13–14, 42, 46, 48, 52, 67, 81, 100n13, 101n1, 110–11n1, 111n6, 114–15n5. *See also* gender, sexual difference
sexual difference, vii, xxv, xxviii–xxx, 14, 33, 49, 52, 57, 75, 81–82, 114–15n5, 117n15
Sibilla di Zani di Laria, 119n16
sign, xxv, 31, 33, 40–41, 58, 64, 75, 77, 79, 93, 97, 100n13, 109n11, 112n6, 113n13, 116n13
Skey, Malcom, 113n11
son, 9, 14, 40, 110n19
Sohn-Rethel, Alfred, 116n14
Sophocles, 7
Spacks, Patricia, 107n23
Stein, Edith, xxvi, 34, 103n8, 109n10

structure, x–xi, xxvii, 39, 42, 45–48, 51–52, 55, 57–59, 62–63, 66, 78, 86–87, 89–91, 93, 98
subject, ix, xi, xiii, xxv, xxvii, 7, 38–39, 41–42, 44, 50, 72, 81–82, 102n3, 109n10, 110n23, 110n1
substitution, x–xi, xiii, xv, xxvii, 26, 51–59, 64–67, 72, 74–77, 79, 81, 89, 97–98, 113n14. *See also* mother: one in her place
symbolic disorder, xxvii, xxix, 7–8, 12–15, 23, 43–44, 49, 56, 58, 66, 67, 87, 103n7
symbolic order, vii, ix–xv, xxvii, xxxiii, 7–8, 14–15, 20, 23, 39, 41, 43–44, 48–49, 57–59, 61–62, 66, 68, 73–74, 77, 80, 82, 87–91, 93–94, 96–97, 100n13, 104n11, 117n15, 118n10, 119n13

Teresa of Avila, 108n3
Teresa di Lisieux or Teresa del Bambin Gesú. *See* Martin, Thérèse
time, 34, 35–36, 41, 63, 73, 77, 79, 88, 90, 98, 117n1
Togeby, Knud, 47
Tomasi, Bibi, 95, 119n14
Totò, 82
Tronti, Mario, xxviii
truth, ix–x, xiv, xxvi, 3–4, 6–8, 9–10, 21–22, 24–25, 27–31, 35–37, 39–40, 43, 49, 63, 69, 71–73, 75–78, 86–87, 94–95, 103n8, 104n11, 107n22–23, 115n9

unconscious, 6, 11, 21, 39, 42, 54, 60, 89
unthought, vii, 28, 105n12

Vannini, Caterina, 108n3
Vattimo, Gianni, xxviii, 12
Vico, Giambattista, 49
Veith, Ilza, 67

Weil, Simone, xxvi, 12, 81–82, 105n12, 118n7
wet-nurse, 48, 118–19n13
William of Saint-Thierry, 105n13
Winnicott, Donald W., xxvi, 36–39, 42, 44–45, 108n4, 108n5, 108n7, 109n10, 109n13
Witches, xxv, 67, 97, 119n16
Wittgenstein, Ludwig, 14, 76, 115n6
Wolgast, Elizabeth, 108n3
women: body against body, xiv, 12, 21, 58; estrangement of, 72, 94, 117n15, 119n13; experience of, xxv, xxvii, 31, 33, 50, 61, 66, 75–77, 88, 94, 97, 101n1, 106n13, 107n23, 113n10; liberation of, 13, 31; politics of, xviii, xxv, xxviii, xxxiii, 6, 11, 33, 59, 70, 72, 82, 89–91, 94, 96–97, 102n3, 107n23, 112n10, 115n5, 118n10, 119n13
word, viii–xiii, 1–2, 5, 12, 21, 29–30, 32, 36, 39–42, 44–47, 49–50, 52, 55–57, 59, 61–66, 70–79, 88, 91–93, 98, 100n13, 101n2, 103n9, 105n12, 110n20, 110n1, 111n5, 116n13
world, ix–xi, xiii–xiv, xix, xxiv, xxvii, 3–4, 6–8, 19, 21, 23, 26, 29, 36–39, 42, 45–46, 49–50, 52–53, 56–59, 63–65, 69–71, 73–75, 88, 96, 101n1, 102n3, 105n12, 106n13, 106n15, 107n21, 110n19, 110n23, 113n11, 117n15

www.ingramcontent.com/pod-product-compliance
Lightning Source LLC
Chambersburg PA
CBHW021144230426
43667CB00005B/251